John Thaw

John Thaw
The Biography

Stafford Hildred and Tim Ewbank

André Deutsch

First published in Great Britain by Andre Deutsch Limited, 1998
Paperback edition first published by Andre Deutsch Limited, 1999
This updated edition first published by Andre Deutsch Ltd, 2002
20 Mortimer Street
London
W1T 3JW

A catalogue record for this book is available from the British Library

ISBN: 0 233 05091 4

10 9 8 7 6 5

Typeset by Derek Doyle & Associates
Printed in Great Britain.

DEDICATION

Stafford: To Janet, Claire, Rebecca, and
my mother Rosemary;
Tim: To Emma, Oliver, my mother Joy, and Carole Anne

ACKNOWLEDGEMENTS

The authors would like to record their thanks and appreciation to all of the many people who have helped in the compilation of this biography. We are particularly grateful of course to John Thaw himself for living such a remarkable life and for giving his time so generously to us for interviews over the years. His teachers, friends and relations from the early days, including Albert Ablott, Fred Eyre, Peter Podmore, Sam Hughes, Alan Watson, Les Potts, Alf Griffiths, Marjorie Cotton, John Knight, Harvey Bryant and Tony Hall were all kind enough to share their memories and to provide invaluable insights. Fellow actors, writers, directors, producers and television executives also helped enormously, but some of them would prefer to remain anonymous, so we would simply like to collectively thank them all. For their support and practical assistance we would also like to thank: Roy Addison, Jerry Johns, Paul Bradley, Robert Kirby, Stuart Darby, John and Wendy Dickinson, Walter and Christine Robson, Gordon Webb, Kenneth Eastaugh, Ivor Newman, John Airey, Roger Davis, Frank Langan, Peter and Janet Garner, John and Pippa Burmester, Shona Johnston, Fiona Knight, Garth and Davina Pearce, Lynn Irving, Mike Bushby, David and Sarah Mertens and the remarkable Smokey. And finally a big thank you to Tim Forrester, Deborah

Waight and Louise Dixon, Peter Mares and all at André Deutsch for their co-operation and kindness.

CONTENTS

PROLOGUE

John Thaw never forgot Christmas 1973. It was the time when events combined to change his life for ever. On Christmas Eve, after a highly emotional courtship, he at last married the love of his life Sheila Hancock. On Boxing Day he had a vital first meeting with the director about playing Jack Regan, the role in *The Sweeney* which was to make him famous across the land. And right over the whole Christmas period his mother Dorothy lay dying of cancer in a Manchester hospice, waiting for the visit from her favourite son.

Elton John was singing 'Goodbye Yellow Brick Road', the Carpenters were on 'Top of the World' and Annie Walker became mayoress of Weatherfield when John and Sheila tied the knot. Peace finally began to spread across Vietnam and President Nixon was struggling to explain his involvement in the Watergate scandal.

John Thaw was thirty-one and well on the way to realizing his heartfelt ambition of successfully building an acting career. He was not yet a star, but he had certainly met and fallen in love with one. The beautiful and outrageous Sheila Hancock was one of Britain's best-known actresses thanks to her hilarious performances in films like *Carry On Cleo* and TV shows like *The Rag Trade*.

It was a second marriage for both of them and, twenty-five years later, despite its single traumatic public faltering, it remained one of the happiest and most enduring. *The Sweeney* changed John's life in another way. He was transformed from just another talented actor who kept popping up on television and in the theatre to a household-name house-wives' heartthrob. His life became public property as steely Jack Regan gripped the nation's consciousness by booting down doors and terrifying black-hearted villains with immortal lines like: 'Get your trousers on, you're nicked.'

But it was also the worst of times for the rising star. For, up in his home city of Manchester, John Thaw's mother Dorothy was coming to the end of her sad life. Racked with agonizing stomach cancer she was passing her last grim days before she died on 2 February 1974 in St Anne's Hospice in Hill Green, Stockport.

Dorothy had walked out of the humble Thaw council house home when John was just seven years old, leaving her husband to bring up John and his younger brother Raymond. It was a dreadful family split that had a painful and lasting effect on all concerned. John's father struggled to combine his life as a long-distance lorry driver with the demanding duties of taking care of two young boys. John, and Raymond, two years his junior, were forced to learn how to fend for themselves at an early age and to survive and grow up without a mother's love when they needed it most.

John has always declined to open up in public about the impact of his mother's decision to leave his father. He has always said: 'My mother went off with another man. It was not very nice.' He has been totally devoted to his proud father and insisted he hardly ever had anything to do with his mother afterwards. He shrugged off offers of sympathy by reflecting that there were plenty of families with both parents in residence who were much unhappier than the Thaw household. However, Dorothy Thaw's decision to leave her husband has had a massive effect on her famous son.

The whole experience helped to forge John Thaw's character. His mother's desertion meant loyalty became for him perhaps the most highly regarded quality in others. He became fiercely protective of his father, who was desolate for a long time after the marriage ended. Yet John was still concerned about the plight of his mother. The awful experience of terribly twisted loyalties at such a young age helped to give him a depth of emotion that other actors could never convey.

Contemporaries have often noted that John appeared to have a terrible angst within him. It was frequently useful professionally but often hard to handle in his personal life. He had lived through watching his father battling to keep him fed and clothed while his mother loved him from a distance. It was an emotional juggling act that produced a character with fierce determination to make the best of everything that comes to him in life. Those close to John Thaw know that his black moods sometimes made him difficult to live with but the inner pain was also a useful tool to use on stage or screen.

The John Thaw story is full of extraordinary chapters. Of how the driven and self-assured young man from the broken home became a celebrity at his secondary school because of his remarkable acting ability. How he made the remarkable leap from the back streets of suburban Manchester to become one of the highest of high flyers in the illustrious history of RADA. And how the remarkable actor became an international star and used his tortured psyche along with the many other intellectual tools in his complex make-up for the most amazing rags to riches adventure in British television.

1

EARLY DAYS

The Second World War was still raging when a happy event pushed the fighting from the minds of two Lancashire families. Lorry driver John Edward Thaw and his pretty wife Dorothy, always known as Dolly, were absolutely delighted on 3 January 1942 when their first son was born. Named John Edward after his proud father and blessed with the beginnings of his mother's curly hair, the baby came into the world at 48 Stowell Street, West Gorton, Manchester after a mercifully short labour.

John Thaw was born in the five-bedroomed home of Cecilia and George James Ablott, parents of his mother. The Thaws and the Ablotts were both large families and they celebrated the arrival of the healthy baby boy together. A birth in the family was always the excuse for a party and many of Dolly's ten brothers and sisters arrived to pay their respects. The good cheer flowed again when John's brother Raymond arrived two years later.

However, some four years later a bizarre tragedy caused them to leave the area. An elderly man collapsed in the street and slumped on to the pavement outside their home. Passers-by briefly revived him and kind Dolly took him into her front room to help him recover, but the stranger's heart gave out and he died on the sofa in front of the fire. The tragedy deeply unsettled Dolly and she pushed her husband to find a new home for the family. When John was five they moved four miles south to Burnage, a suburb which was, much later, to become notorious as the home of the Gallagher brothers, of Oasis fame.

Nevertheless, it was a move upmarket, and the new council home at 4 Daneholme Road delighted both John and Dolly Thaw since it had a garden for the children to play in. And, even better for young John Thaw, it was just a street behind the towering palace of entertainment known as the Burnage Odeon. A visit to the Saturday morning cinema club became the highlight of the week for John and his younger brother. He loved those post-war Hollywood heroes like Hopalong Cassidy, Roy Rogers and Flash Gordon. John enjoyed the excitement and glamour of the big screen, but he was not content simply to sit and watch. The cinema management encouraged the more extrovert members of its audience to get up on stage and try their hands at introducing the programme, as well as providing entertainment during the intervals. Outwardly, John Thaw might have been an ordinary Manchester lad, but inside him burned a desire to entertain, which was ignited when he first stepped on stage at the Burnage Odeon and heard the sound of children laughing at the jokes he had remembered from the radio.

John's father was surprised and delighted when his son contributed gags and impersonations because they went down so well, and soon John and his younger brother Raymond were allowed in free every Saturday morning. Contemporaries still marvel at the cool sense of self-possession with which young John approached an audience.

Sadly not all his childhood memories are so happy. By the time John was seven his parents' marriage was ending. His mother returned to her family in Gorton and the young John and Raymond were left living in Burnage with their distraught father. John's recollections of what happened are painful and brief, to say the least.

He said years later: 'I did not see her again until I was nineteen. It was not very nice. She is dead now, bless her. But I saw her once in 1960 or '61 and that's it.'

As they grew up the bewildered young Thaw brothers were frequently left in the care of neighbours when their father's job forced him to stay overnight away from home. In the days before the motorways criss-crossed the country, a trip to London or the West Country in a lorry could mean two or three days away. The couple from the flat upstairs, Frank and Gladys Bell, used to come down and tuck John and Raymond up in bed for the night. John said: 'We had to go to bed at eight o'clock, after I'd listened to *Dick Barton* on the radio. The back door was always unlocked in those days and Gladys used to come down and make sure we were in bed and that we had had something to eat.

'They were very kind. They used to look after us. They would come down at the appointed hour and make sure we were in bed. Gladys would leave us a glass of milk and biscuits and turn all the lights off. It was nice for us, in so much that we knew Gladys and Frank were just above us if there was any threat.'

The young brothers grew up taking a hand with the housework, even though their father tried to do all he could to protect them from the effects of their mother's abrupt departure. But they all tried hard to help each other and father and sons became very close. John recalls: 'We all mucked in. We had to. It became a way of life and at least it taught us self-sufficiency and self-reliance. We leaned on nobody. As we grew older we learned how to cook for ourselves, but it didn't go much beyond bangers and mash-style food. My memories of those years are mostly of fish and chips and baked beans. The Burnage house was not new but it was a great improvement on Longsight. We even had a little back garden, which pleased my father. My dad would park his lorry outside the flat at night when he had an early start. My brother and I used to love playing behind the wheel.

'Family life is important to us. But then I think it is to most people, whether they've had an unhappy childhood or not. I don't think I was deprived and I don't regret my childhood. We had a lot of love from a lot of people, particularly my dad's family. We felt loved and I think that was the most important thing. I know there were people with "whole" families who were far unhappier than I was.'

John and Ray were like chalk and cheese. 'I was the rough, street fighter sort,' says Ray. 'We used to fight and argue but I wouldn't let anyone harm my brother. Although he was the oldest, I felt he couldn't protect himself like I could and I couldn't stand it if anyone had a go at him.'

The absence of a mother's love seemed to concentrate John's mind on making the best of what he had. An early friend remembers: 'He always seemed older than the rest of us. He liked a laugh and everything, but there was always something held back. He was very self-assured and he always did what he wanted without worrying too much about what anyone thought. He was devoted to his dad and his brother, and as long ago as I can remember he wanted to be in show business.'

When he was just eight years old John would play at

making broadcasts on 'Radio Stowell Street', at the home of his Uncle Charlie and Auntie Beattie who lived at number 82. Charlie had worked on a subcontract at the BBC and brought home a discarded old-fashioned microphone which delighted the youngster. They rigged up a make-believe studio in the lavatory, and young John delighted the family with his hilarious impressions and gag-telling sessions.

The young Thaw brothers' junior school at Burnage was the nearby Green End Boys, where Raymond quickly established himself in the football team and John expressed his first ambitions to act. He soon got his chance. In 1953 Manchester's education authorities decided they wanted to merge Green End Boys with Green End Girls, and to celebrate the amalgamation a jointly produced play was to be performed. Alan Watson produced *Where the Rainbow Ends* with fellow teacher Arnold Wilkinson. Alan recalls: 'When we did the auditions we soon realized John was outstanding. Everybody could tell even then, when he was only eleven years old, that he had real acting talent and potential for the future. It stood out a mile.'

John was brimming with delight and enthusiasm when he landed the main male part of Uncle Joseph, and cheerfully joined in the preparation and early rehearsals in his Easter holidays. Alan Watson said: 'John was already known in the school even then as a budding thespian, and while his brother Raymond was a marvellous gymnast but not at all academic, John was very literate. On the big night, 19 May, which I can remember clearly because my son was born that same evening and I should really have been at the hospital with my wife, John was terrific. Even at that age he was totally convincing as an adult and brilliantly held the whole show together.'

In the classroom John Thaw did not shine during his years at junior school, but he surprised his teachers and delighted his father when he passed the 11+ examination and moved on to Ducie Secondary Technical School (Boys) in Whitworth Park, Manchester 15.

John's own verdict: 'I was very lazy at school. I didn't try hard enough and I hated maths and all the science subjects but I did like English.' As a boy John spent many hours reading. He read *Wind in the Willows* at least eight times. 'I loved that book,' he says. 'And I devoured all of John Buchan and Rudyard Kipling, as well as all the comics and magazines I could get my hands on.'

The performing potential in young John Thaw also revealed itself early on with a bold venture into stand-up comedy. 'I used to do Max Miller impressions down at the youth club,' says John. 'I nicked the jokes and tried to deliver them in his accent. God knows what I sounded like. I must have been about twelve at the time. I didn't really have any ambitions to be a comic, it was just something I could do and I enjoyed doing it. It seemed to make a few people laugh. Although I would be horribly embarrassed now to see the things I did then. I am not an extrovert. In fact, in a crowded bar I would be the last man to be served. But I enjoyed being someone else. I enjoyed putting myself under their skin.'

The audience at school laughed as well, when John took his first ever acting role at secondary school in his first year in the school production of Shakespeare's *Henry IV, Part II*, as Mistress Quickly. He was clad in an enormous white cloak, which brought howls of laughter from some of his classmates, but John took the part very seriously. 'I enjoyed being on stage, being someone else. It was something I just felt I could do. I had a gift for acting and mimicking people. I have always had a good ear for voices.'

Art teacher Alf Griffiths was one of the many people impressed by the acting ability of the young John Thaw. Alf says: 'What sticks in my mind is that on his very first day in school he said he was going to be an actor.' Remarkably, contemporaries all agree that from his earliest days at Ducie, John Thaw had somehow become a celebrity. There was something about the natural confidence of the would-be actor that discouraged mickey-taking. He certainly suffered his share of schoolboy teasing but it was mainly affectionate. John's acting ability was there for all to see and, just like the boys who shone at football or cricket, his undeniable natural ability earned him respect from his classmates.

Les Potts taught PE at Ducie and recalls: 'When John first came to the school he stood out from the others because he was so short and stocky. He went for speech therapy in his first year at Ducie. I was surprised that someone who had had speech therapy as a youngster should go into acting, but I think he was encouraged into the classes because it would help him with his diction. I can certainly never remember John being at all hesitant. The acting seemed to help his confidence all the way through, because although he had a good sense of humour and enjoyed a laugh, I remember him being very, very shy.'

Few first-year kids got into the school play but John's presence virtually demanded a part. History teacher John Lee was a fine amateur actor himself and he always aimed for the very highest standards in school drama. The dedicated teacher spent hours of his own time nurturing dramatic talent and he simply refused to work with young actors who were not enthusiastic. He wanted children who had a desire to act and tended to ask for volunteers rather than go round saying 'I want you' when he was putting a cast together. It was John's burning enthusiasm for acting that first brought him to Lee's attention.

Ducie's headmaster was the wise and benevolent Sam Hughes who well recalls his star drama pupil. 'John had done some acting at his junior school, which John Lee knew when he auditioned him for Mistress Quickly,' said Sam. 'In his first year he had a piping high voice which meant he could carry off the part of an old woman, so he landed the role. He was very good, of course, and in every other year he was there he had prominent parts and was always excellent. He learned his lines perfectly, even though he was never by any means academic at school. It baffled me how he seemed so completely to understand the Shakespearean speeches he was so brilliantly delivering. John was never a show-off and nor was he ragged about his ability. He was always very much appreciated.'

Ducie, in those days, was a very tolerant school. John Lee was an inspired teacher to have in charge of drama and he was never a man to be easily pleased. He was not at all frightened of saying to John, 'It's no good that way. Stop this nonsense, let's do it this way.' He was by no means an easy or pliant man to work for. He could turn his temper on if necessary. John had a great deal of help from him.

John was very popular but he did not court popularity. If people liked him, then that made life marginally more pleasant, if they didn't, well, that was their loss, not his. In most things he was totally laid back. Sam Hughes said: 'When we tried to get rugby started at the school John wanted to take part in the first practice. But he got a bloody nose and when he went home his brother said, "John, you're not doing this again." He also showed no great academic prowess at all.'

The kindly head learned of John's difficult home circumstances by accident. Sam Hughes said: 'John was late to school one day. Quite a bit late, and that was out of character for him. His form master sent him to me because his hand was bleeding and had not been attended to. There had obviously been some sort of accident. The master sent him for punishment but when I asked what had happened John said, "I was opening a tin of beans for our breakfast." I said, "For whom?" He said, "For my brother and myself." I said, "Why was that?" He said, "We have to do it for each other." I said, "Is that because your mother is working?" He said, "My mother doesn't live with us any more." '

The news came as a profound shock to Sam Hughes and he winced as he saw the anguish on the young boy's face as he reluctantly explained his family circumstances. John loathed the idea of anyone feeling sympathy for him and his brother. They and their father had become so close that John refused to recognize any domestic deficiency at all. He had seen his father dedicate his life to making sure the boys were happy and he knew memories of his mother were painful for all of them. So he blocked them out. A schoolfriend said: 'John told me once it hurt if he thought about his mother so he did not think about her. But he didn't tell his father. He thought the world of his dad. He would do anything to avoid upsetting him.

'Mostly he seemed very hard about anything emotional. Except I remember once we were talking about Mothering Sunday and he went a bit misty round the eyes. He just said, "It's all right for you," to no one in particular and stormed off grumpily.'

Sam Hughes clearly recalls what tremendous efforts

John's father made to support his sons. John senior gave up his job as a lorry driver to be a local ambulance driver so he would not be away from home. Sam said: 'He made a lot of sacrifices for John. Without them John would not have been able to go on and achieve what he has achieved. He would have ended up with a gang of muck-abouts.

'John's father fought hard for John to come to Ducie. He arrived at the school two weeks late because he was borderline in his 11+ exam. He was strictly ineligible to go to a selective school until his father insisted he could not have John going to a secondary modern school. And they looked at his exam papers again and decided he was worth considering for a selective place. He couldn't go to Didsbury because they were full so he came to Ducie because we could shove him in.

'John never used his difficult home circumstances to court pity. He took some time to find his feet and decide what he wanted to do. But when he made up his mind his ability shone through. I think we were both lucky. Ducie was fortunate to find John and he was fortunate to find us. Very few of the pupils lived locally. The bulk of them came from our catchment area which was north Manchester. I think John was just about the only boy who came from south Manchester. It was almost by fluke, because his father persisted. There was this arrangement that boys who narrowly failed to get a place at grammar school, should get a place at secondary technical schools like Ducie with the authority paying the equivalent of a fee. And luckily for John, Ducie was much more geared to the arts than the technical side. I don't believe if he had gone into any other school in Manchester he would have had a chance of getting into RADA.'

John's schoolfriends recall a cheery teenager with a mop of unruly curly hair who somehow always managed to look the odd one out. Peter Podmore, a close pal throughout John's schooldays, remembers him as being very like: '. . . the kid in the Persil advert with the grey shirt instead of the white one. He had a mass of mousy-coloured curly hair. I think he probably couldn't afford to get it cut. And at PE when we took our shirts off he was always the one with the dirty vest.'

Of course, unlike most of the other boys, John did not have a mother at home to take care of his laundry. Peter Podmore recalls: 'John never gave a lot away about himself. But I remember once we were messing about, running round the benches in the chemistry lab, and John caught his blazer jacket pocket on a doorknob and it ripped the pocket off. He was really upset about that. Nothing much bothered him and if it had been anyone else he would have collapsed laughing but because it was him, it was serious. He couldn't afford a new one and he didn't have a mum to sew it up again.

'It has always surprised me that John went into serious drama because at school he was a great comedy actor and was always very funny on or off stage. The most popular programme at the time was *The Goon Show* and John could take off all the voices. He was really entertaining. John was great fun and very open with his friends but he wasn't a brilliant scholar.

'His nickname at school was Charlie, because we decided Mistress Quickly's first name was Nellie. And everyone picked up on him being called this in the play and called him Nellie, which he most definitely did not like. He kept saying, "Don't call me Nellie, please don't call me Nellie." We said, "What shall we call you then?"'

He said, "Call me Charlie." And after that we always knew him as Charlie Thaw.'

Peter and John were good friends all the way through school. The only time they fell out was over another boy nicknamed Wriggler, because he was such a little lad. Peter said: 'One day for some reason John was picking on Wriggler and I stepped in and said, "Just leave him alone." John said, "What are you going to do about it?" And I said, "If you don't leave him alone I'll smack you one." He stepped back and looked at me. And then he went through this elaborate rigmarole of very slowly and deliberately putting a pair of gloves on. As if he had to prepare properly for a fight. But they weren't boxing gloves, they were just ordinary gloves. That was just the sort of dramatic thing John would do, even for a scrap in the school yard.'

Young John needn't have bothered with the gloves. 'I hit him once and he went down,' recalls Podmore. 'But we were friends again the next day and it was all forgotten. We spent a lot of time together all the way through school. But John was always a little different. Not stand-offish or anything, just self-contained and a bit different. We used to go into Whitworth Park across the road at lunchtime. We'd be messing around playing football or whatever and John would be reading or rehearsing whatever part he was going to play next.

'We all had girlfriends at school; even though they were technically at a different school we were all in the same building. The girls seemed to change quite a bit for most of us, but John only ever got involved with one girl there, a Eurasian called Alison Lui. She was gorgeous-looking, with short dark hair, almond eyes and olive skin and John went out with her when he was fourteen and fifteen. They were always together.

'He was quite a simple lad who loved acting, and he was a fantastic mimic, particularly of the teachers. Our favourite impression was of chemistry teacher "Terry" Thomas [nicknamed after the popular gap-toothed English actor of the day]. The teachers all seemed to be real characters. One called George Mitchell wore the same suit for all of the seven years I was at school. It was his demob suit. And Maitland was our maths master. He was a big hefty chap who seemed fascinated by machines. He always seemed to have a raincoat on and he would often pull out a crank of a car and say, "What do you make of this?" Barnes used to throw blackboard dusters at us, the ones with the wooden back that really hurt when they hit you. John was a very easy lad to get on with and he was always entertaining. He tried quite hard at schoolwork but I think a big burden in his life was his mother leaving. Deep down I know it bothered him a lot but he hardly ever talked about it. I always felt he found it a terrible problem. I only ever once went to his home. He wasn't feeling very well one day and I went with him to make sure he got home all right.

'He was useless at sport. He was always overweight, and he was never that interested anyway. There were no sports that he got involved in, because he was always fat. But John wasn't bothered; he just always wanted to entertain. He always wanted to make you laugh.'

The absence of a mother's touch at home was keenly felt by young John when he saw his classmates munching sandwiches that had been lovingly prepared at home for them. He solved his own lack of sandwiches in a typically novel and direct manner.

Harvey Bryant was another close classmate at school who recalls this slightly darker side to John Thaw's character: 'The first year we were there we got pally as soon as we started at school. There was a boy there, a nervous character who was very puny and didn't have any friends. He was very frail, this lad, and he was always being bullied so John Thaw decided he would provide protection. John told the lad that if he brought him sandwiches every day he would protect him from the bullies. So this frail lad used to bring him sandwiches for his lunch every day.'

And Peter Podmore remembers: 'We used to run a protection racket which was fairly advanced even if it was completely illegal. I remember we would look after a weedy little kid called Bradshaw in exchange for three-pence a day, which seemed a fair enough deal at the time. It's the sort of thing you'd get kicked out of school for these days. John often got caned, but then we all did. It didn't seem to have much effect. We used to go in the bike sheds smoking. There was always a lot of coughing. And if we got caught we got punished. We never went round worrying about the next time but it certainly hurt. Maitland used a well-worn plimsoll, Lee used a strap. Either way it hurt.

'We had an engineering drawing and woodwork teacher called George Shires. He used to dish out the strap just for things like being late going into class. The girls were on the floor above; but it wasn't a mixed school, they were a different school upstairs. There was an imaginary line across the school yard and nobody set foot across it. If you did you got absolutely slaughtered, the discipline was very strict. Because the girls were upstairs and separate from us we used to do things like go outside and get a dog then let it go and chase it upstairs into the girls' school and see what happened. And we used to throw tennis balls through the windows so we could go and get them back.

'But it was full of rough kids. Moss Side was a tough inner-city area even then. Ducie was a great school for camaraderie but there were an awful lot of villains there. Boys became policemen, crooks or salesmen but we all developed in character.'

In those days there was little in the way of sex education in the school curriculum but at Ducie they hardly needed it. Prostitutes used to ply their trade up and down Denmark Road just outside the school, and the pupils were in no doubt what the ladies were up to. They wore skimpy skirts with black stockings and always seemed to be bursting out of their blouses. Young John was one of the many more confident boys who were not afraid to exchange a bawdy joke with these working women.

Peter Podmore said: 'We didn't need sex lessons in class. That was there in front of your eyes right from being eleven years old. We got it all looking out of our playground. After school we used to amuse ourselves by counting the Durex in the back alley. It was incredible, but it was part of life at the time. Every morning we used to say hello to the prostitutes. We thought we were very grown up talking to these old boilers.

'We were always getting into trouble. We slipped out of school one lunchtime to watch *Jailhouse Rock* in Manchester. It was when we were taking our GCEs. We had a free period all afternoon so at lunchtime we decided if Elvis Presley was on at the Royal we were not going to miss him. There were about thirty of us, including John, of course, who sloped off. Mr Rowe kept us in for that. He was the English master, our form master, and we all got a caning and lines for that as well. Punishment was very strict. The teachers all used to have a cane, a strap or a slipper.

John was never shy as a kid, say his schoolfriends, but he rarely talked about his family. Even as a boy he was not one for small talk. Unless he was launching one of his merciless routines, mimicking one of the teachers, John was largely quiet, often wandering around with his head in a book.

John Thaw's talent was brought out by John Lee. He never married and channelled all his energies into school drama, putting on the sort of ambitious plays that ordinary schools would never have attempted. John was only fifteen when he played Macbeth. The would-be actor worked really hard on that play. He was always very conscientious about his acting, but his final-year Macbeth was special.

He was not laughing the day he was late for the school bus and in his hurry tripped over the kerb and broke his foot. The bones failed to set correctly and the accident left Thaw with the trace of a limp which, years later, has often been noticed by keen viewers of *Inspector Morse*. 'It doesn't hurt,' says Thaw. 'But when I get tired it does tend to drag. I have had people writing in suggesting I am suffering from all sorts of strange diseases.'

Even though he became a leading light in the school plays, Ducie Technical High School was anything but a traditional theatrical breeding ground. It was a hard school and, to some of the younger pupils at least, John Thaw was a hard guy. Fred Eyre, the Mancunian footballer turned businessman and popular author, was four years below Thaw at school and vividly recalls an encounter.

'John was as big when he was fifteen as he is now,' says Fred. 'I was a first year then and scared to death of him and his gang. He came up to me once and ordered me to go to the tuck shop and get him a packet of Durex. I hadn't a clue what Durex was but I knew you didn't chew them and

I was pretty sure you didn't smoke them. While I was wondering about it he whacked me over the back of the head with a dozen pennies wrapped in a handkerchief. I went into the shop for a minute and hung around looking for Durex among the Mars bars and the Wagon Wheels. Then I went out worried that I might get another whack.

'I told John and his gang that the woman had sold out of Durex and fortunately for me they all roared with laughter and rushed off in search of another victim. John was always a guy to avoid in the playground. But then we were amazed when we saw him in the school play. He played Macbeth and I can still remember it to this day. We didn't understand the play at all but it was obvious to all of us that John Thaw was magic on stage.

'He was just fantastic. We all thought acting was a cissy thing to do. People had to be forced to be in the school play in those days. But tough guy John Thaw did it and he had such presence and star quality we just knew he would be a top actor one day.'

John's performance in *Macbeth* was the culmination of a glittering sequence of school plays produced by the dedicated Mr Lee and featuring his ambitious star pupil. Sadly John Lee has since died but his successor as producer, Les Potts, remembers it clearly. 'John was absolutely brilliant in *Macbeth*. He was in every play in every year all the time we were at school and by the time he played Macbeth he was a very accomplished actor. In one part of the play he was on stage on his own when another actor failed to arrive on cue. He was in the loo being rather poorly at the time. As a result John was left on stage on his own with nobody to speak to. It showed the quality of the young man then because somehow he managed to dream up lines that were certainly not Shakespeare, but sounded close enough to the Bard's blank verse to kill time and keep the audience happy. As a result he was able to hold the fort long enough for his fellow actor to recover and I know a lot of people in the audience never even realized there had been a problem.

'Mind you, they say that things always go wrong in the Scottish play. I was stage manager and I somehow managed to cut my finger on John's sword and there was blood all over the back of the stage. I must have just run my fingers across the blade and cut a vein. Still, it all added to the atmosphere.

'*Macbeth* was sold out for a week in our little school hall and some people still talk about John's brilliance. He certainly had the talent, but I believe he owes an enormous debt to John Lee, who helped to nurture that talent. If he had gone to a school that did not place such great store on good drama he might never have made it. John Lee was very proud of what his brightest pupil went on to achieve and I know John Thaw was always deeply grateful to his old teacher.'

Not that John was ever very interested in hanging round for the back-slapping that followed each successful performance. Harvey Bryant remembered that on one of the five nights of the run of *Macbeth*, John insisted on rushing him off for a drink in the Gaumont Bar where the big attraction was a line-up of local prostitutes. Harvey recalled: 'John never had any problems getting served even when we were well under age. We just thought it was fun going to look at all these racy women. Not that we were in the market, you understand. Most people did have girlfriends by then and often changed around quite a bit. But not John. He was devoted to Alison Lui; he only ever really had eyes for her.'

Certainly John Thaw was not always on stage and there was still plenty of time for fun. Harvey said: 'Our physics teacher, Mr Thomas, came in for a lot of mimicking from John. Terry always used to tell us off and finish by saying, "Well, I'm not having it." And John used to take him off to a tee. Yet he always liked John, most of the time at least. One day he was not so keen was when John and I piled chairs up in the corridor outside the physics lab and tied them with a piece of string to the door. It was just before he came to mark the books in the late afternoon. We stood outside and watched through the window as he walked into the room and all these chairs came tumbling down.

'Other times we used to get the caretaker to give us a crate of milk and we would go downstairs to the boiler room with it and sit and smoke and read our books and keep out of everyone's way.

'John was always talking about acting and he was very impressed by Charles Laughton and Albert Finney, whom he reckoned was Laughton's protégé. And I can remember him dragging me along to see them in a play together in the Opera House in Manchester when we were about fifteen.'

But his mother's emotional pull frequently hung heavy over young John. Harvey Bryant remembers: 'John's mother used to work as a waitress at the Shakespeare pub in town and we would often go down there after school to see if there were any sandwiches left. John always seemed to be hungry. His mum seemed very nice. She always seemed to find us something and she was always very pleased to see John.'

Sometimes the visits sent young John into one of his darker moods, as he wondered why on earth his parents couldn't have been like his classmates', who stuck together through thick and thin. He liked to see his mother and bring her up to date with his latest school acting exploits. But he was devoted to his father and he knew it would upset his dad if he learned of the trips down to the Shakespeare. Sometimes he would even try to talk about the past and what had happened to make his mother leave, but she would start to cry and say how sorry she was and he always hated to see his mother in tears.

Harvey said: 'John was always very fond of his dad and he was certainly the apple of his dad's eye but there must have been something there for his mother for him to go down to the Shakespeare to see her. She worked at lunchtimes and when we went down after lessons she would just be clearing up, and we always seemed to get given something to eat from the leftovers.

'He was a good bloke to know and he was very definite about what he was going to do. He used to impress upon me he was going to make it as an actor. He was always saying, "One day I will be on *This Is Your Life*." And "One day it will be Sir John Thaw." ' As he grew older he read widely, not just Shakespeare but modern playwrights, and even about the history of the theatre. The ambition to use his talent for acting as a way out of Manchester grew slowly, but he started to follow theatre news and friends were amazed that he seemed to know exactly who was appearing in which play and which theatre.

One of John's closest friends in his last two years at school was classmate John Knight. The two schoolfriends shared a great enthusiasm for jazz. 'It was the era of the skiffle groups in those days and what really first drew us together was our love of traditional jazz. We both enjoyed listening to Lonnie Donegan and Chris Barber at the Free Trade Hall in Manchester, and our friendship grew from

that. We were fifteen, and at one stage we even had ambitions of starting our own skiffle group. There was another
kid called Peter Black with us. I had one of those old
Dansette record players and my father had a Grundig tape
recorder. We used to get together and play and record all
these bloody awful skiffle records and think we could
emulate them. John and I used to go to jazz clubs and jazz
concerts. It was just in the era when the rules were relaxed
and American musicians were more able to come over here
and John and I lapped all that up. We used to go to the old
Manchester Hippodrome. He had a great sense of humour.
Once, just as we were finishing school, we had some free
time so we organized a trip to Chester. There was a party
of us, girlfriends and all, and we were in a pub near the
city wall and John was sitting in this oak chair very loudly
giving one of the long Shakespearean speeches. In this case
the audience was not that receptive. The landlord threw us
out.

'His home background was very sad. John was always
very careful to do everything he could to look after his
younger brother. I went to their house at the back of the
Odeon cinema in Burnage quite a few times and the
home circumstances were really quite poor. The place
was pretty basic by anyone's standards. But I don't think
John and Raymond were deprived. There was just no
evidence of a woman's touch. The lady upstairs used to
come in and look after them. They weren't totally on
their own.

'As we left school we were very close and he did ask me
to come to London and try to do this acting thing with him.
We used to knock around together all the time. But I'd seen
him acting with the concert parties from the local youth
club. They used to go round old folks' homes and sing and

dance and so on. In the finale all the kids would get these instruments made out of cardboard and mime to Glenn Miller records. John took me along and they put me on the drums. I have never been so embarrassed in my life and that was only at the rehearsal. I knew then that the acting life was not for me. John was very kind but I think he realized.

'John would come up to our house and bring his long-playing records of Laurence Olivier's speeches to listen to and record. My father thought it was very strange that he could switch from skiffle and rock and roll to Shakespeare. John knew all along that he wanted to be an actor. John Lee, the history master, was a great encouragement to John and he would always be in the school plays. But Mr Lee was a very authoritarian figure, a very strong character. We once went on a school trip to Holland and Belgium on a coach and somebody peeled an orange and Lee went mad. He couldn't stand the smell. John didn't go with us; I don't think his dad could afford it. But he learned a lot from Mr Lee. I remember John playing Ben Gunn in *Treasure Island* and he was brilliant.'

John Thaw remembered: 'I knew I had a talent for acting. Everybody told me so at school. I used to go to the theatre with my gran when I was younger to see the variety shows, but I had not seen any legitimate theatre. That was very much for the middle classes. I was a member of the Burnage Community Association concert party, entertaining old folks and going round hospitals. I was a stand-up comedian, would you believe? I wouldn't have the courage now.

'But, coming from that background, I did not know how to become an actor. At first it surprised everyone a little. There was an image of actors being middle-class snobs and very posh. People like us didn't go into that world. I thought, "Damn it. I've got a talent so I can have a go." I knew if I could become an actor I could make a living at it but I did not know how. It was my good fortune to have as my headmaster a great man called Sam Hughes who helped me all the way. First he introduced me to people at my local youth club who explained to me what drama schools were and advised me how to get into RADA.'

The local Burnage Youth Club played a huge part in providing an outlet for the Thaw acting talent. Marjorie Cotton ran the club and remembered determined young John getting the rules of the club relaxed enough to allow his younger brother to come along with him. 'Raymond was only twelve or thirteen and you really had to be fourteen but John was looking after Raymond because their father was away,' said Marjorie. 'John was always very caring about looking after Raymond. He insisted he could only come if we let Raymond come in with him, and we wanted John to come in with us because we soon found out about his talents as an entertainer.'

Ray was always very sporty while John would prefer to listen to long-playing records of Sir Laurence Olivier reciting Shakespeare. 'I used to think he was a bit strange and I'd tell him "turn the bloody thing off",' Ray recalled. 'But he'd ignore me and just sit there and listen.'

The youth club ran a concert party which went round entertaining in old people's homes and hospitals, and even staged a show in a prison on one occasion. Marjorie said: 'John was very funny as a lad and we soon gave him the job of compère. He was younger than all the others but he really grew in stature when he got on stage. He seemed to come alive with an audience. The rest of the time he and Raymond kept themselves pretty much to themselves. You hardly noticed John. But when he was compère you could see star quality shining brightly.

'Because of his family circumstances we helped John out quite a bit. I remember I made his compère's outfit of a black jacket, trousers and tie from old blackout material from the war. It was all fairly do-it-yourself but we put on some marvellous shows.'

Marjorie's daughter Barbara is just a year older than John and she helped him with elocution lessons which further improved his performances. Barbara remembers: 'It was a bit like *The Gang Show*. We would have sketches and songs and John holding the whole show together. Once he got out there on stage we just left him to it. He was completely self-assured on stage. We had lots of talks about what he wanted to do in the future and he always said he wanted to go to RADA and become an actor. He talked to his dad about it and first his dad had told him he couldn't afford things like that and John would have to get a job.

'I was part of a dancing school which also taught elocution and drama, so I finished up giving him elocution lessons and Joyce Palin, who owned the school, gave him drama lessons. Joyce was in the very first six episodes of *Coronation Street* but she came out because she thought there was no future in it! John's dad was not against his son's acting ambitions but he just thought they might be nothing but a schoolboy's pipe dreams at first. Yet he had the foresight to allow him to have some training to see if he really was serious. John knew all the time he was serious.

'There were a lot of contrasts in him at that early age. He did not like any fuss or being extrovert in the normal way. Often when you talked to him it was hard to get any information out of him. He was not a socializer, but when he went on stage he became a different boy. I am a year older than John. When he was fifteen and I was sixteen most of the other people in the concert party were aged from eighteen to twenty-one. Yet even though they were much older nobody ever challenged John's right to be compère.

'The club was open three nights a week – Monday, Wednesday and Friday. This was in the 1950s when we didn't have a telly and John was not into dances or anything. He just loved to entertain. My strongest memory of those days is how protective John was of his brother. He always had to look after Raymond and some nights he could not come because of that. People did not exactly feel sorry for him but they knew he was a lad with a lot to carry, not having a mother at home. Sometimes he would turn up for rehearsals and we would find out he hadn't had anything to eat, so my mum would do a meal for him. And other times she would darn his socks or mend his trousers. Those were the old community days and we were very aware of John's needs and that he had no mum at home. If you talked to John about his family he would just say he had a dad. He never mentioned his mother. He would say, "I haven't got a mother." '

2

RADA

When John left school his acting ambitions were still a vague dream and to experience the real world of work at first hand he took a job as a porter at Smithfield, Manchester's fruit and vegetable market. John recalls wryly: 'I certainly got some encouragement to get into acting from that job, because right from the start I just couldn't stand the pace. I had to get up long before the crack of dawn because it was a four o'clock start and, because I happened to work for the guy who felt he always had to be the last stall to close, we often didn't finish until lunchtime.'

John was paid a pittance. His employers turned out to be among the hardest-working, lowest-paying employers in the market. He lasted eight weeks, his five-foot nine-inch frame occasionally buckling under the heavy potato sacks he was required to hump around. He soon tired of it and went to work as an apprentice for a master baker. The hours were almost as unsocial and John spent his time making doughnuts until the call he had been waiting for came. He was asked to audition for the Royal Academy of Dramatic Art.

John was given the day off to travel down to London to

audition for RADA and, with little money to spare to pay for his fare, it was John's uncle Charlie who volunteered to drive him down to London in his two-tone cream-topped Ford van. John's father and brother Ray also went along for the ride and to give him moral support, waiting outside while John read for RADA's principal, John Fernald.

'Nervous? I was quaking with fear,' John recalled. 'I'd never been to London before, and it was even worse when I got there because all the others waiting for the audition seemed older, richer, and bigger than me.

'I was sitting waiting to go on when one of the students said to me: "Are you frightened?" I nodded. I didn't trust myself to speak. "Don't be," he said. "Just go on stage and look confident. That's all there is to it. Confidence. That's all many of the students here have got." I thought he must be right because he had just passed the audition.' But John's big moment still remains a blur. 'I just remember I was so nervous I could scarcely speak, let alone act.'

John chose to read from *Othello* and called upon the tuition he had received from Barbara Cotton and Joyce Palin. He had learned almost parrot fashion how to declaim certain lines, and put this into practice for John Fernald's benefit. To his delight and surprise, he made enough of an impression to be offered a place at once, although he was, of course, too young. At sixteen he was technically two years under the minimum age limit. 'I lied about how old I was,' said Thaw. 'I was told to tell everyone that I was nineteen and only John and some of the tutors eventually knew what my real age was. I think I must have looked older even then.'

Now that John had won a place at RADA he and his father faced the very real problem of how they were going to pay the RADA fees, which were £45 a term. John's school head Sam Hughes told them both that he would do his utmost to try to secure a grant for him through the education committee of the local Manchester authorities.

'We didn't exactly pull strings with the education committee to get him a grant,' Sam remembered, 'but let's just say that we spoke to the right members at the right time.

'John had done very well to pass himself off as nineteen when he was only sixteen. It was a great achievement. The problem was that the Royal Academy of Dramatic Art was not a university, but it could just about be considered a place of further education. He wouldn't have got a penny in grant if he had wanted to go to a school of dance, but an academy for acting was a different matter. It was quite a loose system in those days and one which scoundrels like myself could exploit!

'Fortunately there were members on the education committee who were interested in drama, and one old lady in particular.'

Councillor Gladys Lord was the woman who was to prove instrumental in helping John secure a grant. Luckily, John's father had come to know Mrs Lord through driving her around for the Duke of York Hospital in Burnage where he worked as a chauffeur. And as it turned out she was the same Mrs Lord who had judged a local talent competition some four years earlier, when John had won by singing 'I've Got a Lovely Bunch of Coconuts' in what he thought was a Cockney accent. John's dad had kept her up to date on his son's progress on stage in the school plays.

So when Sam Hughes spoke to her about his school's production of *Macbeth* and suggested she might like to see it, she was intrigued to hear that John Thaw was playing the lead and said she would be delighted to come to the performance. Hughes even arranged for her to be picked up and driven to the performance and then taken home again afterwards. 'After that I was sure that when the question of a grant came up for the boy who played Macbeth so well, she would speak up for him,' said Hughes.

John Thaw was duly allocated a grant to enable him to enter Britain's leading drama academy. He was given £7 a week by the corporation to live on and to this day he remains profoundly grateful to his headmaster for all his efforts to secure the money.

'Sam Hughes never let on what my real age was when he helped to wangle me that grant,' says John. 'That was part of being lucky. I'll always be grateful to Sam Hughes. Of course it was an unusual choice of career for a lorry driver's son from Manchester but my dad, bless him, backed me all the way. He always had the attitude for both Ray and me that he would support us whatever we chose to do. A lot of kids would have been laughed at if they had said they wanted to become an actor, but dad was terrific. "If you blow it," he would say, "you can always come back but at least you've had a go." '

So it was with a mixture of fear and excitement that John Thaw presented himself at RADA in Gower Street on 29 September 1958 to begin the autumn term as a C division student. He knew nobody in London and because it was cheap and convenient he booked himself into the YMCA hostel in Great Russell Street, which was just a short walk away from RADA.

'I arrived for my first day dressed like a typical Teddy boy,' he remembers. 'It was 1958 and I wore jeans with tight ten-inch bottoms, crêpe soles, a silk scarf round my neck and my hair in a typical duck's bottom cut. The other kids in the class took one look at me and were petrified. I don't know whether they thought I'd pull a knife on them or what. But they just avoided me.

'It was very frightening and hard at first. It took me three months to come to terms with it all and at least one term to fit in. There were only about two people who spoke to me during that first term – the others were frightened of me while I was frightened of them. I was terrified, while they were all saying, "Don't go near him, he'll hit you." '

It was a bewildering and deeply unhappy time for John. He felt isolated, lonely even, and because he was either ignored or regarded with such evident disdain by fellow students he frequently questioned whether he would ever fit in at RADA. Other students treated him with the utmost suspicion and made it clear they resented having a Teddy boy from up north in their midst.

'I was working class and from the north and the majority of students were middle- or upper-class southerners, very self-assured with their stylish casual clothes and sweaters thrown over their shoulders,' says John. 'I'd arrived in my drape jacket and tapered trousers, which was the only way I knew at the time. But to them I was like something out of a zoo or a Martian.

'It took quite a while for me to throw out the tight trousers and the drape jackets and lose my accent. Mind you, the accent didn't matter so much because there were others in my class – like Tom Courtenay – who had a strong accent and the reason I was there was to sort it out. You don't leave home if you are not determined. I had come down to London to make my mark.'

Within weeks of his arrival at RADA John's acting ability was put to the test when he was assigned roles as

Guiderius in *Cymbeline*, as the Banished Duke in *As You Like It*, and as Lopature in *The Cherry Orchard*. He had been thrown in at the deep end and he remembers literally shaking with fear performing in *The Cherry Orchard*. The principal of RADA had positioned himself in the front row of the audience and John was almost overwhelmed by his presence. 'He was sitting six feet away and I couldn't keep the cup I was holding from rattling,' he said.

The young John Thaw found it hard at first to pick up what he was being taught and he admits his studies suffered from all sorts of complexes about his background and his Manchester accent. His first end-of-term exams were, he says, less than satisfactory and the director, Clifford Williams, called him into his office and in a Welsh accent which John described as 'thick as a couple of pounds of Caerphilly cheese' told him he was worried about his Manchester accent!

John returned home to Manchester for the Christmas holidays, gloomily fearing the worst. He wondered whether RADA would have him back for a second term. Even if they did, he was disillusioned enough to wonder whether he even wanted to go back. He spent an anxious fortnight at home before he received a letter saying he had passed his exams. It was the perfect seventeenth birthday present and now his mind was made up. He was going to return to London and make every effort to work hard and show his contemporaries just what he was capable of. By the time he returned for his second term he felt more at ease and his complexes had largely disappeared.

His old schoolfriend Harvey Bryant noticed a marked change in John when they met up in Manchester for the first time since John had become a RADA student. They arranged to meet outside the CIS offices in Miller Street, where Bryant had started work, and John was bubbling over with enthusiasm about his new life in London. He suggested they go for a coffee so he could tell Bryant all about it.

The two old schoolfriends repaired to a Wimpy bar in Oxford Street and Bryant was astonished at John's behaviour once they had made their way through the door and sat down. 'We were sitting at a table inside when John suddenly stood up in the gangway, shouting at the top of his voice, impersonating some young actors he had met up with in a pub in London,' Bryant remembered. 'He mentioned Peter O'Toole and Albert Finney, who of course were little known at the time and, using the most flowery language and gestures, John gave an impression of how the actors spoke. He did it all extremely loudly.'

Bryant remembered that John's extraordinary impromptu performance brought an instant hush to the packed Wimpy bar. 'John did it all as though he was on stage and I was embarrassed because he was speaking so loudly everyone in the Wimpy bar turned round to look at us,' said Bryant. 'Having talked like that at the top of his voice, he then sat down and was his quiet self again. It was extraordinary.'

Returning to RADA for his second term, John studied hard and his distinctive, natural ability, coupled with a new-found confidence and self-belief, swiftly set him apart from most of the other students. His talent for acting was there for all to see, both students and tutors alike, and it helped him gain a measure of respect from his peers, who were starting to look at him in a very different light.

John gradually settled down at RADA and began to make friends and explore a little more of London life. The capital was a forbidding, sprawling, unfriendly place to

John when he first arrived in the autumn of 1958 and he rapidly discovered that simply surviving was far from cheap. After a brief spell at the YMCA he moved to digs in Grand Avenue, Muswell Hill, and says: 'At first money was so tight that I had to make do every day with a cheese roll. If I went to the pub one night I didn't eat the next.' Later he moved to a more central flat in Cheyne Gardens in Chelsea. 'I shared with other students with whom I felt I had something in common. I felt I was in competition with the others because I just had to be better than they were. That was very important to me.'

These new friends opened up a whole fresh view of London for John. The capital was changing and the influence of youth was everywhere. When the fifties began there were no 'teenagers'. As the decade drew to a close there were five million in Britain – and Britain knew it. Teenagers had their own distinct culture. Rock 'n' roll was sweeping young men like John Thaw and his friends off their feet, the London coffee bars were full of youngsters gathered around jukeboxes drinking frothy coffee in glass cups dispensed from gleaming Gaggia coffee machines, and everyone under eighteen seemed to know three chords on a guitar.

In a Soho basement coffee bar called The Two I's, young singers like Harry Webb and Tommy Hicks were being transformed into Cliff Richard and Tommy Steele, as Britain's answers to Elvis Presley, while some of John's slightly older friends were enjoying the revival of traditional jazz at Humphrey Lyttelton's club at 100 Oxford Street.

It was an exciting time to be young and John gradually came to experience the vibrancy of London in the late fifties as he found his feet and left Manchester and his roots further behind. John made friends with contemporaries like Tom Courtenay and Sarah Miles, who would later go on to find fame in the movies, and Geoff Hinsliff who many years later became a familiar face in *Coronation Street*. By the end of his first year John had progressed smoothly through the Middle C stream to Upper Middle 1C and his student acting experience had broadened to encompass playing Aune in *Pillars of Society*, Baptista in *The Taming of the Shrew*, and Florizel in *A Winter's Tale,* as well as Matthew Skipps and Hebble Tyson in *The Lady's Not For Burning*, and Sir Andrew Aguecheek in *Twelfth Night*.

From the outset John's enormous, innate talent was apparent to the RADA teaching staff. The RADA principal's report at the end of John's first year reflected the academy's enthusiasm at finding such a gifted fledgling actor in their midst.

John's report went to the City of Manchester's education department on 23 July 1959 and it began with minor quibbles from voice coach Clifford Turner. 'You must still concentrate on bringing your voice forward and aim for a less woolly quality,' wrote Turner. 'You have improved where details of speech are concerned.'

Apart from that faint criticism of his vocal delivery, John's report thereafter could scarcely have been bettered even if he had chosen to write it himself.

'Young Thaw is a natural, a born blissful character actor with phenomenal theatre instinct,' enthused Teddie Grant, although, interestingly, Grant had originally begun his assessment with the words 'Old Thaw' but had crossed the phrase out to replace it with 'Young Thaw'. He was either aware that John had joined RADA as a sixteen-year-old or, like so many, believed John to be much older than he really was.

Grant continued: 'Things which actors acquire through prolonged contact with audiences he seems to know already – the comedic effect of an increase in volume, a pause, a look, an expert piece of timing: these he uses with sureness, not as technical experiment. More important since they could never be acquired are the compassionate humanity and delight in absurdity which inform his comedic slant on people. I have the feeling that his talent is more versatile than he himself believes, and I'd like to see this proved since this type-casting world may well keep him waiting thirty years before permitting him to play most of the parts he already essays so promisingly.'

Peter Barkworth, who took a RADA class on audition technique, was equally glowing in his assessment. 'A good strong actor who has worked well this term and to good effect,' Barkworth reported. 'When he acts with continuity (keeps thoughts going in the pauses) and when he eschews a certain physical over-emphasis, he has immense power. I hope his yen for over-acting has gone for good. Certainly I have noted a great improvement. For the future he will, I think, have to watch that vocal mannerism (a way he has of biting words) and a tendency to be sullen are used only in roles for which they are suitable otherwise he will limit himself unnecessarily. I have derived great enjoyment from his work this term.'

Another teacher, John Broome, noted the physical presence John was already bringing to his acting. 'A most interesting term's work,' wrote Broome. 'You are showing you have the power to communicate in the simplest of gestures and, though you have certain restrictive tensions, your emotional and expressive control is excellent. Your physical control now develops with ease, and when in complete command of yourself, you carry tremendous conviction.'

Only one section of the later part of the report, a typed and unsigned appreciation of John's first stab at Shakespeare at RADA, was less than glowing. 'Played Sir Andrew in *Twelfth Night*,' it read. 'John shows signs of developing into a useful character actor and is acquiring a feeling for the size and style of Shakespeare. He still has to learn to appreciate the shape of a scene and his part in it – i.e. where it needs lifting as a new thing begins – but this will come and is only lacking at the moment, I think, because he concentrates on the reality of his own performance. There is still a slight veil over his acting but I think this again is the "small truth" – he must work to enlarge himself and through that his acting. Good work.'

The overall view was highly encouraging and John's end of year report signed off thus: 'I am delighted with what you have achieved in your first year. You are becoming good in many styles of acting and you have won a complete victory in the battle for standard English.'

Returning on 5 October 1959 for his second year, John was placed in the Upper Middle 1A class. But after playing Tubby in *Hobson's Choice* it was clear he was was making such rapid headway that, unusually, he was promoted in November mid-term to Finals 2, thereby skipping Upper Middle 2 and Finals 3. It was no mean achievement, especially as some of his direct contemporaries were failing even to last the course.

In the spring of 1960 John returned to RADA as a Finals 2 student for his fifth and penultimate term. One day, while passing one of the classrooms, he happened to look through the glass-panelled door to see his friend Tom Courtenay being put through his paces in a singing class.

Courtenay was doing his best to warble 'Who is Sylvia? What is she?' much to John's amusement. But there was method in Courtenay's apparent madness.

'There was a big musical coming up, set in the East End with the leader of a gang of Teddy boys as the main part,' Courtenay recalled. 'It would have suited John wonderfully, being as he was in those days a bit of a hard case. But he said: "No way am I going to sing." I sang "Who is Sylvia?" and got the part and John had to make do with a part in *Paradise Lost*.'

John had warmed to Tom Courtenay enormously from the moment they first met. Like John, Courtenay came from humble northern roots – he was brought up in a back-street house in a tough neighbourhood near the Hull docks. His father had been a trawler painter in the docks and, after an accident, then worked in the paint store at the fish dock. There was an instant affinity between the two young drama students, although Courtenay had arrived at RADA by a very different route from John. Courtenay had failed his degree at University College, London, and had then been awarded the Leverhulme Scholarship to RADA. But there was nothing superior about Courtenay's demeanour and he was quick to explain to everyone that his somewhat aristocratic-sounding surname belied his background. 'Despite my posh name, it's really French for short-nose,' insisted Tom, down-playing it all.

John's path might have taken a very different turn if he had won the role of the Teddy boy in the musical. Courtenay, with his hollow-cheeked, brooding good looks, made such an impression in it that he was snapped up for the Old Vic.

But John played Mammon in Milton's epic with his by now customary competence and earned the plaudit 'A strong and imaginative performance' from James Evans on his end of term report. John followed up by adding Teiresias in *Antigone* and Chorus in *Alcestis* to his list of RADA roles and won still more praise. 'Outstanding performances in both plays, but then John Thaw is an outstanding student in every respect, including discipline and application to work' was the assessment which took him into Finals 1 for his sixth and last RADA term.

As usual John studied hard right to the end and his swansong as a RADA student was to play Mephistopheles in *Faust* and Michael in *The Knight of the Burning Pestle,* which had his teachers in rapture. 'There is only one word to describe his acting: brilliant!' wrote Martin Spenser of Thaw's Mephisto. 'He gave a mature, masterly perfor-mance which, considering his youth, was simply staggering. John owes his success also to his discipline and extremely hard work. I have no doubt that he has a bril-liant future in front of him.'

The principal also predicted big things. John Fernald wrote in John's final report: 'You made a remarkable finish to a remarkable Academy career in your last term and I have no doubt that you are going to do very well in your profession. The very best of luck to you.'

As he left RADA at the end of his two-year course John was able to reflect quietly on the remarkable direction his life was taking. Many years later, while filming an episode of *Morse* in Italy, John was in reflective mood and cast his mind back affectionately to his RADA days. 'Acting was the only thing I could do. I could never have done anything else,' he said. 'I still sometimes wonder how did I get here, from a council flat in a suburb of Manchester to a beautiful luxury hotel in Italy? I had a lot of luck and a gift that I was given.

'Acting is not something I learned to do. I am just very

lucky that I was given the opportunity to use that gift. A lot of fifteen-year-old lads would have been laughed at if they had said they wanted to act. Dad just said, "If it doesn't work, come back. We're here." Dad knew I was interested in acting because he had seen me acting in the school plays and youth club concerts. We always thought the idea of being an actor was something that happened to other people, not us. But when I got the chance to go to RADA it just sort of made sense. It was something I could do so I went. Ray was different. He was a very outgoing physical person who loved sport. I got the mickey taken out of me, certainly, when I went back to Manchester, but not in a nasty way.'

3

FIRST BREAKS

John left RADA on 23 July, 1960. Like Tom Courtenay, he gained an Honours Diploma but he had always had a competitive edge and he also won the coveted Vanbrugh Award for the best performance by an actor for his Mephistopheles, and the Liverpool Playhouse award too. The awards meant that while still in his last term of training he was able to look forward to a guaranteed start to his working career, as a contracted actor in repertory in Liverpool at £10 a week. 'At last I was a professional actor and still only eighteen,' said John.

However, Liverpool proved to be a chastening experience. The critic on the local Liverpool evening paper rarely had much good to say about John Thaw. Worse still, she also wrote reviews for the *Stage*, the much respected actors' weekly trade journal. It irked John that other members of his profession would be reading his poor reviews until a fellow actor managed to help him put it all in perspective. He reminded John that the great American actor John Barrymore used to say that he never believed the critics if they were bad, so why believe them when they are good?

Intriguingly, while at Liverpool John played his first role as a policeman – complete with a false wobbly moustache.

But with characteristic single-mindedness John left Liverpool after six months, as he put it: '. . . under a bit of a cloud. I walked out on the contract because I felt I was picking up bad habits from some of the older actors.'

Returning to London, John spent a few riotous months sharing a flat in Highbury Fields in north London with his old RADA friend Tom Courtenay and another rising young actor, Nicol Williamson. Like John, Williamson had left school at the age of sixteen and was just down from rep in Dundee and starting to make something of a name for himself.

The flat was in a battered but elegant house in Georgian Islington, entered through a hall stacked with odd pieces of reserve furniture and pictures, leading to the uncarpeted stairs. It was dominated by a splendid sitting room which had a hit-and-miss smartness about it, with gilt paint on the picture rail and a potent shade of blue on the walls. Otherwise it was the usual young bachelor apartment, with endless cups of tea and something stronger provided for all manner of visitors calling at irregular hours. Some were aghast on opening a door to one of the rooms to find it was simply a junk room where the three of them used to chuck anything that appeared surplus to needs at any particular moment. Realizing their domesticity left something to be desired, they agreed to hire a cleaner, with all of them chipping in to pay him a generous five shillings an hour. However, as the cleaner was himself a drama student, he spent most of his allotted time chatting to them all about their dreams and aspirations, and too little time busying himself with a duster and mop.

The flat-sharers' one requirement of the cleaner was that he step carefully around the toy electric racing car set, laid out on the floor of one of the rooms specifically emptied to accommodate it. Williamson had acquired it one day and he, Thaw and Courtenay spent many a happy and raucous hour racing the cars round the track while laying bets on themselves and each other. When they all tired of it they simply packed it up and unceremoniously dumped it in a dustbin.

Inevitably, three good-looking young bachelors sharing a London pad had little difficulty in attracting women, but none of them had the money to become real hellraisers. Williamson kept his flatmates entertained with his flair for brilliant mimicry and lively conversation. They all enjoyed spending time together listening to records on the gramophone. Tom Courtenay especially enjoyed classical music and he helped encourage John to appreciate the works of Bach, Sibelius and other great composers. It was a grounding in classical music which was to be a lifelong influence on John.

Like many a young man, John's initial interest in skiffle had also given way to the hit records of the day by American rockers like Elvis Presley and Buddy Holly but now, thanks to Courtenay, his ears were opened to symphonies, concertos and opera. John also had the pleasure of working with Courtenay in a TV Playhouse production called *The Lads* and later he had a small role in the 1962 film that was to make Courtenay's name, *The Loneliness of the Long Distance Runner*.

John was genuinely thrilled for his friend when Courtenay was chosen to star in Tony Richardson's film about a disturbed Borstal boy from an unhappy home in the Midlands who, as a natural-born runner, is selected to represent Borstal in a race against a public school team.

At their home in Highbury the trio liked nothing better than to sit up into the small hours, talking about various aspects of their profession, fuelled by a couple of bottles of wine if they could afford it. 'Sometimes I drank too much beer or played too much poker,' John recalled. 'But I think one of the wildest things we did was to buy that electric racing car game.'

An increasingly regular visitor to the flat was an attractive young woman called Sally Alexander whom John had met while she was working at the Saville Theatre as an assistant stage manager. Generous of spirit, Sally was fond enough of them all to tidy up behind them and to try to bring some semblance of order to the flat.

To his joy, John had found himself at the Saville Theatre in 1963 at the age of twenty as understudy to the great Laurence Olivier in a production of *Semi-Detached* by David Turner. He could scarcely believe his luck at being able to observe such a revered actor at work at such close quarters. There were lots of actors whose work impressed him but John, while determined to copy no one, admired Olivier above all. *Semi-Detached* proved a fascinating experience for him. 'I learned a great deal from Olivier. He was so relaxed on the stage that you actually forgot that he was an actor playing a part,' he said.

Olivier recognized the young man's talent, befriended Thaw and gave him a very generous twenty-first birthday present. 'It was a silver cigarette case from Asprey's,' recalls John. 'And because his character in the play was called Fred, he had it inscribed "To John Thaw from another Fred." I was very moved because he even had his own handwriting copied for the inscription.'

It was just after John Thaw's birthday that he found himself pressed into action on stage, as the great man took a week off suffering from gout. John had already stood in for him once at short notice but now he had to take on

Olivier's role for a whole week. For a young man to be asked to step into Olivier's shoes was daunting enough, but it also required John to carry off the role of a sixty-year-old man. At twenty-one John may have looked many years older than he actually was, but this was clearly a formidable challenge.

John and Olivier were both in the lift ferrying them between the stage and the dressing room when John anxiously enquired of Olivier whether he should age himself for the role by powdering his hair silver. Olivier smiled and said thoughtfully: 'Do as I do, baby. Amaze yourself with your own daring.' John recalled: 'That is something I have often thought about since and I can't always do it. But as I have got older I think I have become more daring.' On the day John was due to take Olivier's place on stage he was thrilled and touched to receive a telegram from him which said: 'Most affectionate thoughts and good wishes for tonight. Good luck . . .'

For John Thaw, *Semi-Detached* also provided the even more momentous meeting with Sally Alexander, who was a year younger than him. Her father was a successful financier and she was brought up in a large house in Richmond. Her affluent background was a world away from John Thaw's less privileged upbringing. They were immediately attracted to each other and the young couple fell enthusiastically in love and were married within the year.

On one of his trips back to Manchester John recounted to Harvey Bryant how he had fallen head over heels for Sally. 'He talked about her so excitedly,' Bryant remembered. 'He said the family had a holiday home in the Bahamas. I honestly didn't know whether to believe him. All this talk of the Bahamas – it was just another world to me.'

John and Sally married in June 1964 and had a honeymoon in Corsica before moving into a small house in
London's Notting Hill Gate. He wanted to put down roots
in London, build a home life and a secure base from which
to launch his career as an actor. John felt marrying Sally
was the best thing that had ever happened to him and they
both believed they had everything going for them. For the
first time since his mother had walked out of the family
home when he was a child, John Thaw at last had a woman
who really loved him and it was, he told friends, a truly
wonderful feeling.

As it turned out, 1964 was an important year for John.
At twenty-two he married, set up home, and, almost like
an extra wedding present, landed his first major television series – *Redcap*, a thirteen-part drama about the
Military Police produced by ABC TV, the company which
provided ITV programmes in the Midlands and north at
weekends.

Redcap was devised by Jack Bell, a former navy man
who was by now an enterprising journalist working on
the *Daily Mirror*. In his role as a television correspondent
on the paper, Jack realized that the Military Police was
one area of detective work which TV had not covered
before. Television viewers had seen local and national
police forces at work, and had been let into the secrets of
Interpol, but the activities of the Royal Military Police
investigators – the British Army's 'CID' – would, he felt,
be a fascinating subject for TV drama. Their work was
akin to that of the CID and their training was very similar
but the chief difference was the vastness of their field of
operations, which would give the scriptwriters plenty of
scope.

'Ironically, as soon as I'd dreamed up the idea for *Redcap*

I immediately had reservations,' said Jack. 'I wondered whether the Military Police was a dirty word for people who had been in World War Two and mostly thought of them as guys who had harassed them when they were on leave. So I decided to go and find out what the Military Police were about today. I approached the top brass and they said yes, good idea, give this man Jack Bell every co-operation. In fact the head of SIB, the Special Investigations Branch of the Royal Military Police, was so helpful that he actually came on board the production as consultant.'

At that time there were only 120 NCOs and 20 officers serving in the SIB throughout the world. The lowest rank was that of sergeant and Jack Bell originally visualized having two main characters in the series. 'NCOs obviously couldn't investigate officer crime,' Jack explained to the TV drama bosses. 'It would need an officer for that. But whether it was for economic or other reasons ABC TV went for just one main character, Sergeant John Mann, and that was John Thaw in the only starring role.'

At nineteen John had made an appearance in BBC TV's police series *Z Cars*, but now he was cast as a highly trained military policeman who ruthlessly investigated soldiers' misdemeanours from Aden to Hong Kong. At one stage there were grandiose plans to film on location in Cyprus and Malaya but production went ahead without, as John Thaw drily put it, 'ever straying very far from the Teddington studios'. The farthest they actually ventured was the military town of Aldershot, but, in its own way, *Redcap* broke new ground on TV, giving viewers an insight into how the SIB operated all over the world, wherever units of the British Army were stationed. Assignments included tracking down a soldier who had gone absent without leave, investigating a murder in Berlin and tackling drug trafficking in the Far East. A number of writers with army experience contributed to the series which gave it authenticity.

John threw himself wholeheartedly into the role. He started going to a gym to work out before rehearsals but found he was so tired by lunchtime that he had to pack it in. He darkened his hair to give Sergeant Mann a meaner look and worked long hours at the studios in Broom Road, Teddington, then travelled wearily home to put his feet up on the chaise longue and learn his lines for the following day while listening to his beloved Bach.

At the tender age of twenty-two John Thaw was at that time the youngest leading man entrusted with carrying a major drama series on British TV, and he was made more than aware of the responsibility resting on his shoulders. Halfway through filming the very first of thirteen episodes, the producer warned him in no uncertain terms that he was less than pleased with the way things were progressing. He ordered John to think hard about the way he was handling the role and, chillingly for John, told him that he had better shape up and show a marked improvement or he would be sacked.

That stark ultimatum made such an impression that John experienced a very real fear in the pit of his stomach during the filming of each episode. He wondered if at any moment he was about to be given his marching orders. 'He was newly married and he had taken on the responsibility of a house, and the worry of it being snatched nagged away at him,' said a member of the *Redcap* production team. 'But he wasn't about to let this chance go lightly. It brought the best out of him.'

John worked hard to bring Sergeant Mann to life on

screen. He gave him an aggressive streak when dealing with soldiers, but an altogether gentler and more compassionate side to his nature when dealing with the wives and families who had lost loved ones.

Redcap was generally well received by both critics and the public alike and was soon sold to Australia. The *Daily Mirror*'s TV critic Kenneth Easthaugh hailed John as a very bright new TV star. He wrote: 'John Thaw in the starring part of Sergeant Mann, an army detective, is a rare and welcome example of a very young actor being treated responsibly on TV and given the lead in an important production . . . and living up to it. Thaw is one of TV's best finds. He has a mind in excess of his experience and years. He has the gift of all the best actors – he makes it all look so easy.'

A second thirteen-part *Redcap* series produced by John Bryce also fared well and gave Jack Bell special satisfaction. He had originally taken his idea for *Redcap* to Rediffusion and the London-based midweek ITV company had turned it down. 'Now that it was a success they were only too happy to screen it,' Bell said.

The second series was launched on 2 April 1966 on the full ITV network and it benefited greatly from following on in the ITV slot vacated by the hugely successful spy spoof series *The Avengers*. With an audience of around 20 million bequeathed by the bowler-hatted Steed and the leather-clad Emma Peel, *Redcap* was able to capitalize on the popularity of one of the top TV shows of the sixties.

The impact of such success on John Thaw was considerable. As the only resident star of the series, his face rapidly became familiar to millions of viewers for the first time. He was none too sure he liked it, especially when he was confronted by three labourers in a Liverpool pub. 'They said: "Are you the bloke in *Redcap*? A little so-and-so like you?" Luckily I was able to talk my way out of it, explaining that I was only acting.'

With *Redcap* providing John with regular work for the first time he was able to acquire his first car. He bought a convertible Triumph Vitesse from his father-in-law some six months after he and Sally married. 'I can't remember what I paid him,' said the actor, 'a few hundred pounds, I think. But it was a good deal. He liked me and he just happened to be selling it. When I was at RADA I couldn't afford a car but by this time I was working for a television company. It was a very fast car, it had six cylinders, it was heavy on juice and infamous for rust.'

John was no mechanical genius and did not claim to know much of what went on under the bonnet. All he knew was that he loved driving that car around with the hood down. It was certainly the kind of car his *Redcap* fans would expect to find him driving. 'That Triumph was a lovely car and I really enjoyed it,' he said. 'It had red leather seats and a black hood which we put down for about three days a year.'

After twenty-six episodes of *Redcap* John was ready to move on to other things. When filming finally finished he took the cast and crew to the pub around the corner for farewell drinks and generously picked up the tab for the night's alcoholic intake.

John and Sally had been married for a year when Sally gave birth to a daughter. They agreed on the name Abigail for their baby girl, as they both felt it sounded very feminine. John was thrilled at becoming a father and he dutifully traded in the Triumph Vitesse for a Cortina GT once Abigail came along.

As a family everything seemed set fair for Mr and Mrs Thaw. 'I was twenty-two when I started *Redcap* and I felt I knew who I was, where I was going and who was going with me,' John was able to reflect. 'When Abigail was born, everything in the garden looked beautiful from where I sat.'

However, within two years he and Sally realized their marriage was over. When it became clear there was little point in staying together it was John who unhappily moved out, sadly observing later: 'We were just too young. I was saddened by the sense of failure but it was the right decision.' Apart from her stint at the Saville Theatre, Sally had had virtually nothing to do with the theatre and her interests had become increasingly academic during her marriage to John, whereas outside of the family, acting was by now John's life. 'I think it was difficult for her to understand when I came home shattered at the end of a day's filming or rehearsing. It's hard to explain to someone who doesn't actually know what it's like.'

The break-up of his marriage was a traumatic experience for John. He had gone into it with such high hopes and good intentions and now it was over. All through his childhood he had felt the need for his mother's love and now the love he and Sally had shared had evaporated.

On top of the emotional upheaval, when John and Sally split up he had serious financial worries. 'Money was my first concern,' he recounted. 'When I left Sally there was a big tax bill to pay – a demand for the *Redcap* years for which I had made no provision. I'd spent the money and I was now paying for the house in which I no longer lived, keeping Sally and the baby and having to fend for myself.'

It was a frustrating time for John and when he wasn't working he would wander around Kensington Gardens, getting more and more angry at having to wait for the next role to come along. He wondered why it was that other young actors less talented than himself seemed to be in employment. In the afternoons he whiled away the time watching TV. He was acutely aware he needed a home and he needed to move on from *Redcap*.

In desperation he rang his old friend Nicol Williamson, who was in New York at the time, and explained his predicament. Williamson told him he had just taken a furnished flat to rent in Bloomsbury in central London, and generously said that, although he had not yet seen it, John was welcome to pick up the keys from the agent and move in. 'That's friendship for you,' said John.

Returning to the bachelor life again was far from easy for John. He felt humiliated when he gathered up his dirty washing one day to take it to the local launderette. As he walked in and began unloading his socks, underpants and shirts into a machine, he realized he was the only man there among half a dozen Cockney women, one of whom recognized him at once from *Redcap*. 'Washing your smalls, Sergeant?' she enquired sarcastically.

'There was a cackle of laughter all round,' said John, 'and I'd never felt so embarrassed in my life. To them I was still Sergeant Mann of *Redcap*, intrepid tracker of men, now washer of smalls. Very funny. But not to me.'

Happily, when he returned to London Nicol Williamson proved to be a real tonic for John. He was always full of energy, loved playing practical jokes, possessed a sharp wit and a sparkling sense of humour and he did his best to lighten a depressing time for John. The two friends had plenty of fun nights out together, but with the shadow of the Inland Revenue's demands hanging over him John was unable to share Williamson's fondness for regularly dining out in style at the Ivy, the famous London restaurant patronized by showbusiness personalities. Williamson was by now a star actor, having won rave reviews for his London stage role as seedy, shabby, lecherous solicitor Bill Maitland in John Osborne's play *Inadmissible Evidence*. 'The trouble was', said John, 'that Nicol was a big star and I wasn't. And where his idea of a night out was champagne and oysters, mine was a couple of drinks in the pub and fish and chips on the way home.'

It was inevitable that John would eventually tire of the gipsy existence he had endured since he had moved away from Sally and Abigail and he was relieved when he was finally able to find a London flat of his own. It may have been only sparsely furnished with a bed, a chest of drawers and some easy chairs, but at least he had somewhere to put his collection of records, and it was a place he could retreat to, shut out the world and settle back with a Scotch and listen to his favourite works by Mozart, Elgar and Bach.

Ironically work soon took John back to Manchester and no fewer than five starring roles in a major Granada TV series, *Inheritance*. This was the story of life in a Yorkshire wool town from 1812 to 1965, adapted from the novels by Phyllis Bentley, and John played members of five generations of the Oldroyd family, each one from the age of twenty to thirty-five and each one enjoying differing fortunes.

During filming John was able to stay with his father, who had by this time moved to leafy Marple in Cheshire. He experienced little nostalgia for the Manchester of his childhood and felt himself almost a stranger in the city where he had grown up. The Mancunians treated him differently and John noticed there was now a barrier between himself and the people he used to know. 'But it's not my barrier, it's theirs,' he said.

Old pals and acquaintances were uneasy about the way John no longer spoke like them and John admitted that at first he found it frightening to discover he had lost all his old friends. But he felt that to excuse himself for going down to London and trying to better himself was not the way to try to bridge the years.

Although John's marriage was over he made every effort to see as much of little Abigail as he could. He adored her and at weekends he would collect Abigail in his blue MG convertible, which she called Bluebird, and drive her up to Manchester to see his father. John's dad had married again a week before Abigail was born. He had kept his word that he would not remarry until his two sons were standing firmly on their own feet. He had felt that to introduce another woman into the lives of his boys would complicate matters for them.

Abigail would come to look forward to the journeys she made with her father. She would chatter away happily while he listened to his favourite tapes of Sibelius and Jacqueline du Pré playing Elgar's Cello Concerto. En route they'd stop for Cornish pasties and a Mars bar and there was always a joyful greeting from John's father awaiting them when they reached Manchester.

Abigail was with him one day in 1969 on a visit to her grandfather when John received what turned out to be a momentous telephone call. It was the offer of a part in a stage comedy by Leonard Webb, opposite Sheila Hancock, in which they were to play lovers. He was required back in London that very afternoon to meet her. As he jumped into his MG and headed back down to London, John was not to know that his life was about to

change for ever. He met up with Sheila and they agreed
they would do the play together. Its title was *So What
About Love?*

4

MEETING SHEILA

Sheila Hancock's first visit to the theatre was to the Holborn Empire in London to see *Where the Rainbow Ends* performed by the Italia Conti School, with her sister Billie playing Will-o'-the-Wisp. Sheila was a patient in Great Ormond Street Hospital for Children. She recalled: 'The vision of my bossy sister transformed into a dainty sprite with gossamer wings gave me a lasting belief in the magic of the theatre – and a violent nose bleed.' She was eleven.

John Thaw's first acting role was playing the leading role of Uncle Joseph in the Green End School, Burnage, version of *Where the Rainbow Ends*. A schoolfriend in the audience said: 'John was just incredible. I'll never forget that night. When he went on the stage he became another person. It was like Clark Kent turning into Superman in the comic.' He was eleven years old.

The two productions might have taken place ten years and 200 miles apart, but the youthful experiences forged at the time made a lasting impression on both actress and actor. One of the strongest bonds between the couple, who celebrated their twenty-fifth wedding anniversary on Christmas Eve 1998, is their lifelong love of their craft.

Sheila recalls a momentous first meeting: 'If I'm honest

the first thing I noticed about him when we worked on stage together is that he was very sexy. We didn't get together then, of course. But we circled round one another a bit. I was married at the time anyway. Still, I did think he was a very sexy man. But he was also rather rude and surly. I have taught him a few manners since then. The title of the play did seem appropriate! I've been saying 'So What About Love?' ever since over the washing up.'

John was instantly attracted to the forceful, older actress who, he was delighted to discover, was every bit as talented and down to earth as he was. He said: 'I enjoyed working with her very much because we seemed to share the same sense of humour. But the play had to come off early when her mother fell ill and Sheila had to be with her.'

The stars made more of an impression on each other than they did on some of the audiences. *Sunday Times* theatre critic Harold Hobson's uncharitable verdict on Hancock was: 'Unbearable to the eye and unendurable to the ear.' And he did not appear to like John Thaw even as much as that, declaring of the future Inspector Morse that he: 'Dreaded his every reappearance on the stage.'

Reviews apart, the couple were intrigued by their meeting but neither of them was looking for a new relationship. John was at last beginning to get over the trauma of the collapse of his first marriage and starting to put his life back together, and Sheila was then still married. John felt he was improving as an actor and he had at last found somewhere permanent to live in London.

'For the first time since my marriage broke up I felt a sense of security. I had a retreat where I could listen to music of my own choice with maybe a Scotch in hand to help me unwind. I am very much a home bird and I like the feeling of shutting the door on the outside world.'

Then, in 1971, Sheila Hancock's husband Alec Ross finally lost his long, grim battle with cancer and died. The couple had been desperately close for nearly seventeen years and their daughter, Melanie 'Elly' Jane, was just seven years old. To add to Sheila's sense of isolation and despair her mother and father had also tragically died. She felt extremely alone. 'Up until then,' said Sheila, 'there had always been a man in my life. To begin with my father, then my boyfriend, whom I married. Being on my own took a great deal of adjustment.'

John Thaw had known Alec and was well aware of the immense emotional burden Sheila had borne over the years. They met again at a dinner party given by a writer friend. 'For old time's sake,' he said later, 'I invited her out to dinner. And from then on the relationship began to grow.'

Unlike Thaw's first wife, Sheila came from a working-class background very similar to his own and they thoroughly enjoyed each other's company. Both had struggled to fulfil their acting ambitions in untheatrical households, and then gone on to feel horribly out of place at RADA. Most important, both had come through the ordeal with flying colours. Their earliest conversations were a heart-warming realization of so many shared feelings and experiences. However, with a broken marriage just behind him, John was wary of starting a second serious relationship. But gradually John and Sheila became close. Sheila insisted: 'John is a terribly shy man. He always says I leapt on him but that wasn't true at all. I suppose I must have made the running but it was he who asked me out in the first place.

'Some time after my husband had died he contacted me and we went out for dinner so he had made that much effort. But after that I think he would have sat there dumbstruck for ever if I hadn't taken charge.'

Sheila found John refreshingly straightforward. His sympathy over her recent loss was direct and sincere. Even though he was a gifted actor he never put on a performance. Sheila described him as: 'A straight-down-the-road person. Early in our relationship he suddenly looked at me with those blue eyes of his and said, "Why do you play games?" And immediately I realized I didn't have to put on a show for this bloke.'

In the beginning they did consider living together. But John says: 'We abandoned the idea because we wanted a baby if we could and we didn't think it was fair for a child to be brought into a world where society, even now, can frown on children born outside of marriage. It's not so much adult society as the society of other children who, consciously or unconsciously, can be cruel to one another. I wouldn't let any child of mine face the possibility of such an ordeal, real or imagined.'

Sheila Hancock, typically for a woman whose humour has helped her through some difficult emotional times, put it more simply. 'Imagine your daughter going to school and saying, "My mum's going to have a baby", and the teacher saying, "Oh, I didn't know she had got married".

'I suppose we drifted into marriage, almost solely for the sake of the girls – Melanie and John's daughter Abigail from his first marriage. They wanted us to be a family, and I think they both liked the idea of being bridesmaids. Neither John nor I was particularly keen on the idea, because we didn't feel it would make any difference to us. But I knew he was right for me and even though the timing was not perfect, I didn't want to take the risk of telling him to come back in a couple of years and then to find he was with someone else.'

Sheila certainly impressed Abigail. They first met when Abigail was eight and in the bath. Sheila wafted in wearing a glamorous red fox-fur coat, accompanied by the sophisticated aroma of very feminine perfume, and charmed the youngster. She pushed off her coat and knelt down to entrance Abigail by pretending to be a crocodile snapping away at her feet. Sheila told her all about her own daughter Melanie and how she hoped the girls could be friends.

Her thoughts and concerns about the future were, curiously, almost exactly mirrored from the other side of the relationship. By this time, although John had thoroughly enjoyed his bachelor status and knew a couple of families of married friends who used to ask him round for dinner and line him up with possible dates, he was very cautious about committing himself. Gradually these glimpses of domestic bliss had their effect and he began to want to settle down again. He was often depressed by his all too brief visits to see Abigail who was living with her mother, and the urge to have a family of his own grew and grew. John said: 'I set out very consciously to win Sheila. She was a very eligible lady. Attractive, vital and intelligent. To me she was just too good to lose. I thought, "I want her to be with me." And so, as I say, I set out to win her. And I did. Luckily.

'I didn't actually say, "I want to marry you," for some time, but I used to say, "We mustn't break this up – we must go from strength to strength," as it were. And then one day it just happened. I loved her so much. And when you love somebody like that you very much want to be with them as long as you can foresee. We were in a restaurant in Regent Street when I asked her to marry me, and to my pleasure and surprise she actually said, "Oh all right. We might as well." '

There was also the age difference to consider. John says frankly: 'Sheila is ten years older than I am. But then, as everyone knows, I look ten years older than I should and the age difference did not, and does not, matter. It is irrelevant.' Sheila did consider the difference but he dismissed her reservations. She said: 'My generation were children during the war and have something missing from their make-up. John's generation have an inner confidence, a maturity, and are definite about their attitudes to life. He is an extraordinary person. I depend on him and he on me. I think if I had been an anonymous person I might have lived with him, but I didn't feel strongly enough about it. When he asked me to marry him, I agreed. When I make my mind up to do something I do it quickly.

'The marvellous thing is that he and Elly Jane hit it off perfectly. I couldn't have considered anyone she didn't approve of.' They married on Christmas Eve 1973 at Cirencester. 'A Christmas present for each other,' laughed John.

Sheila said: 'I was appearing in a West End show that night and we thought we would keep it quiet, but we didn't realize that the Cirencester Register Office was right opposite the local paper. We were driving back to London when we heard our wedding announced on the news. When we arrived there was a wonderful party arranged by the cast.'

The night before the wedding Sheila told Elly Jane what she was planning to do. The youngster burst into tears and the bride-to-be thought her daughter did not want them to marry. 'Then I realized she was crying with relief,' said Sheila. She said, "Oh, Mummy. I was hoping you would." Elly Jane and Abigail were both present at the simple fifteen-minute ceremony.

Sheila's show was the comedy *Absurd Person Singular* at the Criterion Theatre and the run prevented the couple having a honeymoon, but Sheila said afterwards: 'We had a lovely Christmas with the kids and we hope to move into a new home in Chiswick before long.'

John soon decided to adopt Elly Jane as his own daughter. He was aware that if anything happened to him Elly Jane would have no claim. 'I couldn't have that, could I?' he said. 'After all, everyone else in the family was called Thaw and it didn't seem fair she should be the odd one out. I said to her, "Do you know what adoption means? It means I become your father, not just Mummy's husband, and you'll have to do what I tell you." She laughed and seemed to like the idea. "Oh good," she said. "I've got a dad again." '

Foremost in John's mind at the time was the comparison with his own childhood and painful memories of a mother who was not there to tuck him up in bed at night. And these memories were further brought into focus at that time by the fact that, up in Manchester, his mother Dorothy was coming to the end of her life. Racked with agonizing stomach cancer, she passed away in St Anne's Hospice in Hill Green, Stockport, on 2 February 1974.

The funeral was a desperately sad affair. On a dull February day in Gorton Cemetery with the temperature hovering just above freezing, seventy-five-year-old Cecilia Ablott shivered as she watched the coffin containing her fifty-two-year-old daughter lowered slowly down into the freshly uncovered grave, to join the casket containing Dorothy's father.

Other members of the ageing Ablott clan glanced towards the nearby gates of the overgrown graveyard as the vicar, with more sad ceremonies to perform later that day, hurried through the formalities. 'He's not coming,' muttered Dorothy's brother Albert under his breath, bitterly realizing that one of Britain's best-loved actors had missed one of the most important dates of his life.

John Thaw's cancer-stricken mother had been buried without even a fleeting appearance by her successful son. 'And a bloody good job, too,' Albert said quietly to his wife Edith. 'If I had got hold of him I would have given him a good hiding.'

The tragic early end to the troubled life of Dorothy 'Dolly' Ablott was strictly a restricted family affair. Neither John nor Raymond was there to pay his last respects. And Albert still feels angry when he recalls the day his sister was finally laid to rest.

'Dolly was a wonderful woman, bright and bubbly and full of life. Until she was cruelly cut down by stomach cancer. She was ill for over twelve months. First she stayed with my sister in Longsight, near where we were born, but then she went into hospital and finally to the hospice.

'The family wrote to John to tell him his mother was dying of cancer and we asked him to come and visit her. We wrote again when she died, to tell him the details of the funeral but he didn't come.

'In the end the family had to organize everything when she died. There was no insurance or anything, so we paid for the funeral. It was cheaper to put her in the family grave than to open another new grave, so that is what we did. Three years later my mother died and that is where she went as well. It was a very, very sad day.

'Dolly thought the world of her famous son. She might have split up from John's father when John was only seven, but she still followed his life and his career closely. She always kept photos and cuttings about John with her and often got upset and cried when she talked about what had happened.'

Since he burst to fame more than thirty-five years ago, John Thaw said very little in his many interviews about his mother, other than that she left the family home when he was seven and his younger brother Raymond was five. John briefly described his mother going off with another man and insisted that he hardly ever saw her afterwards.

Albert remembers it all rather differently. 'Those stories are a load of garbage,' he said. 'Absolute garbage. For years I have wanted to say something to put things right. When John was born I was twelve years old and I often used to stay at their house to keep Dolly company when John, her husband, was away. She hated being left on her own in the house and my mother used to send me round so there was someone else at home.

'Certainly they split up. But Dolly didn't go off with another man. She moved back in with my mother in Longsight. The marriage just was not right. She couldn't stand John being away from home so often. Even before he became a lorry driver he worked nights at Fairey Aviation, and although they had been happy when they first married they just drifted further and further apart. So in the end they parted and she went back to our mother.

'But she did not abandon the boys. She paid a neighbour to be a sort of child minder and look after them and she went back a lot to see that they were all right. She cared about them a great deal but she just couldn't live with her husband any more. Later she did meet another man, a salesman called Alan West. They got married and ran pubs. First they had the George and Dragon in Manchester and when that was pulled down they moved to the White Horse in Prestwich.

'As a lad John was quite bright and took after his mother, in that he was outgoing and constantly had a cheeky smile on his face. He was always taking people off, even as a very little boy.

'John used to come into the George and Dragon a lot, to cadge money from his mother. I used to work in the bar then and I remember seeing John coming up from London when he was at RADA to get money from her. She always gave him five or ten pounds, which was a lot in those days. And she would always be very upset when he had gone. It's just not right of John to make out that his mother didn't care and that he never saw her. Not right at all.

'My sister was desperate to see John all the time she was fighting cancer but he never bothered. He has always ignored all Dolly's family, our side. When he was on *This Is Your Life* nobody from our side of the family was invited. It is as though he has blacked out a whole part of his life.

'John Thaw's mother was a wonderful woman. And he looks so like her. The fact is that his mother loved him very much. She was a real worker and did all sorts of jobs before she and Alan got the pubs. She did waitressing and managed cafés and even ran a boarding house in Wales for a time. She had lots of pictures of John around her house but she was so sad that she never got to know John's daughter, Abigail. Her own grand-daughter and she didn't even know her!'

Albert's anger is understandable and it was considerably increased soon after Dolly's funeral. 'Dolly did not leave very much,' says Albert. 'But she did have six gold rings. She knew towards the end that she was dying and she wanted our six other sisters to have a ring each. Just to remember her by. They weren't particularly valuable, I'd be surprised if they were worth more than a thousand pounds altogether. But my sister Cecilia stepped in. Off her own bat, without consulting anyone else, she told John that his mother had left these rings for him. He, wanting a keepsake, I suppose, arrived at the house soon afterwards in a chauffeur-driven car and collected all the rings from Cecilia, then he got back into his car and drove off.

'I have been angry for many years that the famous John Thaw should lead people to believe he was dumped and left on the doorstep by his uncaring mother, because it was not like that. I have not wanted to say anything before because I was very friendly with John's father. He was a very nice fellow and we have had many a drink together over the years. I didn't want to upset him, but he died in 1997. And now I am suffering from cancer so I probably have not got that much longer myself. So I feel it is time the truth was told.'

John Thaw was always reluctant to discuss his painful relationship with his mother but his brother Raymond insists John did make a last emotional visit to see her some months before she died. The reunion took place after he had been appearing in a play in Manchester. One of Dolly's sisters sought him out backstage after the show and told him of his mother's deteriorating health. 'Your mum's dying of cancer. Could you pop in and say "Hello"?' John's aunt enquired anxiously. John's initial reaction was to decline the invitation. However, as he sat behind the wheel on the long journey back to London he changed his mind and found himself drawn to the house where his mother was wasting away. He stopped the car, knocked on the door and inside found the woman who had brought him into the world lying in bed and close to death.

'You'll have to forgive me for what I did,' she murmured. 'I know you think bad of me but it was just something that happened. You can't turn the clock back,' she whispered to the actor as tears welled in his eyes. After twenty minutes together they said their last goodbyes and never saw each other again. That final reconciliation was almost more than John could bear. The sad spectre of his mother's life always rested heavily on his shoulders.

Dolly Thaw went to her grave bitterly regretting the hurt she had caused to her two young sons by walking out on her marriage. But she knew she could not bear to stay at home any longer. She always refused to talk about what had gone wrong at the heart of the relationship, but it was clear that she felt guilty that she had left. A friend said: 'Sometimes she would go quiet and her eyes would mist over and I knew she was thinking about the boys. She never minded giving John money when he came in the pub. Sometimes she couldn't really afford it but afterwards she would sigh and tell me, "It is the least I can do." '

Dolly followed John's career closely and, many times, when he was in the theatre in Manchester, she would go and sit quietly sobbing in the audience, in proud and painful awe at the remarkable talent of her older son. She was very upset one night when she got talking to some people and plucked up courage to tell them that John was her son. They laughed unkindly and wouldn't believe her. Dolly's life was full of sadness. Her second marriage ended just as unhappily as her first when her husband walked out on her, leaving her in poor health and with very little money. In the end she had nothing and was forced to go and live with her sister before the final fight with cancer.

John Thaw was determined that his children should have two parents to love and rely on. The family lived in a comfortable Victorian house on the banks of the Thames in Chiswick, west London, and also had a pretty little bolthole of a country cottage in rural Gloucestershire. The man who was brought up in an exclusively male house-hold now found himself the only man in a feminine home. Not only Sheila and Elly Jane, but also frequent visits from Abigail, and then, the next year, the arrival of John and Sheila's own daughter, Joanna Suzy. John noted wryly more than once that even the dog and the cat were female. He had been known to break out in mock hyster-ics at home and scream: 'I'm surrounded by women. Help me.'

The marriage received the full support of Elly Jane and Abigail, who quickly became firm friends as well as step-sisters. Elly Jane felt John was wonderful and has happy memories of him using his drily perceptive sense of humour to make her laugh. Because she and Abigail were so enthusiastic about their parents' match, they experi-enced none of the rivalry of ordinary sisters. They were both only children who were delighted to have a happy new enlarged family. Elly Jane, who attended the presti-gious London public school St Paul's, certainly went through a rebellious phase as a teenager and found John the calming influence when she clashed with her mother. Abigail went to Pimlico Comprehensive, where some pupils later called her Sweeney Girl, but the reflected fame was something of a double-edged sword. Some pupils would tell her how wonderful they thought her father was on television, but others would become jealous and she did suffer some bullying.

This was one of the happiest periods of John Thaw's life. Friends recall that at long last the tense edge often lurking just beneath the surface of his temperament seemed to subside during the early years of his marriage to Sheila. John said: 'Now this is going to sound romantic, but then I am a romantic, I love Sheila and the children very much, and when I work, when I act, I'm doing it for them. Whatever success I have relates to them. I am proud of them and I want them to be proud of me, too.'

With a flash of real insight he said: 'Marriage to Sheila has worked, and worked well. We're mature people, both practising actors who understand each other's problems. I love Sheila's sense of humour, her caring for causes that matter and her sensitivity where other people are concerned. I'm not like that. When I'm working I get very involved, very frustrated, very uptight at times. I am self-absorbed and not always aware of what others are suffering. Sheila can snap me out of it because she understands. She encourages me and helps me to get things in perspective. She has had her bad times, very bad times, and I have known what it is to be intensely unhappy. So you tend to enjoy and savour the good moments together. You don't take anything for granted.'

By the time their daughter Joanna was born John Thaw was carving out his alarming new identity of Detective Inspector Jack Regan in *The Sweeney*. Some of his favourite precious off-duty moments were spent wheeling Joanna in her pram through Chiswick Park which raised a few eyebrows from *Sweeney* fans.

John was disappointed when one youngster called out to him: 'You shouldn't be pushing a pram, Regan!' He said:

'That incident was sad because one day that kid will be pushing a pram, and it's a pity he should think you can't be both tough and a pram pusher.' Not that he ever remotely envied Regan's hard man reputation. John explained: 'Some of the toughest men I know, some of them policemen in fact, are the gentlest and most sensitive of people. They've got families. They push prams and they wash dishes and yet they can be very tough.'

Much more important to the couple was their ability to share the ups and downs of high-profile acting careers. Sheila said: 'It is a hard old business so it is very nice to have somebody who is sympathetic and is on your side.'

In some senses, though, John Thaw and Sheila Hancock do have different temperaments. She is lively, full of spirit and never slow to fight for the cause of the moment. He is quieter, withdrawn almost, with a much more laid-back attitude to life. John recognizes that dark moods can take him over but he made a conscious decision to try to stop himself getting down, and over the years friends insist he mellowed considerably. Some of the anxiety came from deep unhappiness over his mother and also from his determination to succeed as an actor. John set himself astonishingly high standards professionally. As a younger actor he would stay up half the night worrying whether he was doing his work well enough. He read the script over and over, learning his lines and struggling to convince himself that he truly had found the core of the role. Consequently he was sometimes grumpy the next day. When he was doing *The Sweeney* he would be handed three pages of script to learn in half an hour. The pressure was enormous, but gradually he learned to deal with it more easily. 'Mind you,' he said. 'I'll never match Sheila for sheer effervescence and get-up-and-go zing. I don't know where she gets her energy from. I've always been prone to certain lethargy when I'm not acting. My maxim is, "Never do today what you can do tomorrow." ' Age and experience softened some of the urgency which used to drive John Thaw.

John believed a shared sense of humour was one of the greatest strengths of his life with Sheila. They laughed at the same things. And John said: 'In the main we like the same sort of music and art, though I like more pop music, all the old-fashioned stuff like Van Morrison and the Rolling Stones. Sheila can't stand them.' A love of opera bound them together and they were regular patrons of Covent Garden and Glyndebourne. 'For me, when it's well done, opera is the best form of theatre,' said John animatedly. 'We love *La Bohème* and weep buckets over it, but if you said to me, "What opera would you take on a desert island?" it would have to be something by Mozart.' Sheila and John loved to lose themselves in an evening of Mozart or Puccini and he has been known to stand at home, conducting like von Karajan in front of the Berlin Philharmonic. 'Years ago we had a holiday in Austria and Germany and we went to Beethoven's house and to Schubert's birthplace. It was beautiful. I'm very fond of Schubert. As you can tell, we're heavily into the Romantics.'

In spite of her long years of experience and remarkable success as an actress Sheila is a self-confessed worrier. Particularly over first nights. In 1980 she became terribly worked up over the opening of *Sweeney Todd*. She recalled: 'Seeing my white face and trembling hands on the morning of the first night, by which time I was convinced I had lost my voice and certainly did not know the words, my husband suggested a walk in Richmond Park. During the previous sleepless night I had frantically read Stanislavsky's advice on stage fright in which he suggests concentrating on the other actors' eyes and the feel, smell and colour of objects around you. In the park I realized I was sick when I startled the deer by clinging to the rough bark of a tree, staring dementedly at my husband, simply unable to move away, the rest of the park being much too frightening.'

At times like that it is certainly helpful to have an actor as a husband. The couple understood the stresses and strains of life as a busy and successful actor, although they used different methods for learning their lines. Sheila uses a tape recorder while John just read from the script. Sheila said: 'Whatever jobs we are offered, we have always sat down together and worked out how it would affect the family. Usually it has meant me turning down work. I often felt that our children could do without me less than they could do without John. I accept that. If you want to be a hugely successful actress you don't have a family, but then you don't have the joy of kids.

'It is so rewarding to see them blossoming and growing up. To see them coming up against things that we came up against and to be able to give them advice from your own experience. When they first had boyfriends I always seemed to like the ones that did not last. For a time I spent my life consoling boyfriends who had been given the push. That was my role in life, picking up the pieces.'

John certainly stepped back from involving himself too deeply in teenage romances: 'I don't vet my daughters' boyfriends. I make comments and of course they take no notice. I am not at all strict but then again that comes from my father because he was never strict with us. Whatever he told us to do was for our own benefit, for our own good, and that is what I have tried to do with the girls. You can only advise, you can't make them do things.'

Richmond was always a favourite area for the Thaws and John and Sheila loved to try to find time for a quiet walk by the river. She said: 'There are too many people there, but if it's a really nice day I can't resist. I like the wildness of Richmond Park, even though it is ruined by aircraft virtually landing on it. My favourite walk is away from the crowds. I love the smell of the earth, my feet on the earth. I walk on my own or John comes too if he feels like it. It's not a ritual.'

Joanna, the youngest, never minded the endless travel that is the price of success as an actor or actress. She loved staying in hotels, and the more plastic they were the more she liked them. Her 'absolute favourite in the world' was the Holiday Inn in Birmingham. She loved all the free goodies like soap, shampoos, bath foam, tea, coffee and shower caps that a night's accommodation provides. Sheila said: 'She was only momentarily confused once by a small plastic carpet beater which I decided was something strange for tired businessmen. Joanna was convinced it was a fly swatter, undaunted by the protest that no fly could possibly enter this hermetically sealed world. John concurred with her, surmising that it had been delivered in error and a lot of people in a Holiday Inn in Cairo were probably equally confused by their consignment of plastic rain hats. Abigail and Elly Jane have had their moments in hotels, too. My husband and I were rather confused by the size of our bills at the end of each week in a hotel in Melbourne when we were appearing there, only to discover that while we were at the theatre and their grandad believed them to be asleep in the next room, they were in fact ordering massive meals from room service.'

The best times for John Thaw were always those at home with his family. The Chiswick house was kept family-oriented and free of routine. Sheila always insisted: 'John is the best cook in the family. He would often prepare Sunday lunch for all of us. But he is a bit of a temperamental cook. He doesn't like us around when he is cooking. He prefers us out of the way once we have prepared the vegetables. If I'm cooking I like everyone around in the kitchen to help and chat.

'We have absolutely no routine in our house on any day. We do as we feel. If we have food in we cook. If not we go out or get takeaways from the local Thai, or Chinese, or Indian, or fish and chips. Chiswick has everything. If we go out it will be for an Italian meal, or an old-fashioned roast, or French.'

The couple had always been equal partners in the marriage. Sheila said: 'If one of us is working the other one will have been to the shops. Whoever is free will go to Marks and Spencer or Sainsbury's. I couldn't exist without their ready-cooked dishes. But on Sunday if the family is here we would cook a joint of beef or lamb – and I would just have the vegetables.'

For pudding the family often share the dish which has become known to them as John Thaw Crumble, blackberry and apple with ice-cream or ready-made custard. Before they sold the Chiswick house, Sheila said: 'We have a lovely old apple tree in the garden, very ancient, wizened and bowed over. It's quite a rare breed and fruits every year with sharp apples like the old days.'

In Chiswick the Thaws spent much time with their close friends and neighbours, the Briers family. In fact John Thaw's flair for cooking extends to the garden and Richard Briers noted: 'John Thaw's barbecues are definitely major productions. John is a fantastic actor and great fun to be with but he is also a remarkably fine cook, especially an outdoor cook. I was with him the night he bought a new barbecue. We were outside, of course, and suddenly we had the most torrential rain. John is a very determined man. You have to be in this rotten business of ours. He was trying everything to make this thing light. We tried paraffin, we tried petrol, we tried gin. In the end, being a physical coward myself, unlike John who is very brave, I was in the doorway out of the rain. And eventually after about two and a half hours he managed to get this thing alight. And if you haven't tasted John Thaw's sausage in paraffin sauce then you haven't lived.'

5

THE SWEENEY

Few British television programmes have broken the mould in quite such abrasive fashion and with quite such dramatic impact as *The Sweeney*. For nigh on twenty years, right from the BBC's genteel days of 1955 when Jack Warner as village bobby George Dixon greeted *Dixon of Dock Green* viewers with a matey 'Evenin' all', British television had traditionally portrayed policemen on TV as benevolent heroes and pillars of rectitude.

But on 2 January 1975, the eve of John Thaw's thirty-third birthday, an altogether different kind of policeman burst on to the screen and it was patently clear that helping old ladies across the road was not exactly his forte. Detective Inspector Jack Regan was not even in the usual league of decent detectives. He was rough, tough, aggressive, sadistic even, a hard-drinking womanizer and foul-mouthed. Yet when it came to beating crime he had a habit of getting results – with violence if necessary, and it frequently was. Then once the punch-up was over, the villains had been handcuffed, and the squeal of burning tyre rubber had died away, Regan was off down to the pub with his colleague Sergeant Carter to celebrate, and to nurse his sore knuckles in readiness for the next gang of armed robbers who dared to try to mix it with the tough-est cops in the Flying Squad.

Millions of viewers got the shock of their lives as they saw Regan, played by John Thaw, stumble out of bed horribly hung-over and borrow the car of the girl whose bed he had just vacated. Regan was off to work and minutes later he was hurling a villain up against a wall, seizing him by the throat and snarling: 'We're the Sweeney, son. So if you don't want a kickin' . . .' It was brash, pacy, compelling and so unexpected it made for electrifying action-packed television.

Even the *Daily Telegraph* was fulsome in its praise of the opening episode. Television critic Richard Last said *The Sweeney* had all the look of a very superior police thriller: 'I doubt if Scotland Yard will relish a new TV detective inspector whose idea of interrogation is to get the suspect against a wall and massage his head a bit,' he wrote. 'Yet as played by John Thaw and the deceptively innocent-look-ing Dennis Waterman, they were both entirely believable, a world away from the cardboard characters of most ITV police serials.'

Before long *The Sweeney* was setting new standards for realistic fights, dramatic car chases and crackling dialogue, and it was to make John Thaw one of the biggest British TV stars of the seventies. During that decade there was no better TV copper.

To his surprise and horror, the show was also to turn John Thaw into a sex symbol. Within weeks of *The Sweeney* hitting the screen, shoals of fan letters began arriving regu-larly at Thames TV's studios. If confirmation was needed that female viewers found John Thaw and Regan sexy, the 150 Bunny girls at London's Playboy Club in Park Lane soon provided it. Seven weeks into the series the Bunnies voted John top of their Bunnies' Valentine poll. John's reward, as well as being the top Bunnies' pin-up, would have been a kiss and honorary membership of the club. However, his agent tactfully turned it down, stating it wasn't quite John's image.

The Sweeney was developed from an idea by writer Ian Kennedy-Martin who had written a play called *Regan* after watching *Z Cars*, the BBC series created by his brother Troy. Euston Films, set up by Thames Television at the beginning of the 1970s as a subsidiary company to produce television and film drama, subsequently turned *Regan* into a thriller for ITV's *Armchair Cinema*, a series of ninety-minute movies made exclusively for television.

Kennedy-Martin, who had worked with John Thaw on the series *Redcap*, was friendly with a detective in the Flying Squad at the time and had heard of the dissatisfaction some officers were expressing about the new order of management which was being established among London's police. He took into account the winds of change blowing through the Flying Squad around the time Sir Robert Mark had become Commissioner of the Metropolitan Police: how the new regime now comprised committee men and memo writers, and how detectives were being asked to do their job from a desk in Scotland Yard rather than mixing with their underworld contacts in East End pubs. He duly came up with the idea of putting a tough maverick cop who bends the rules in among the new disciplinarians.

Kennedy-Martin never had any doubt that John Thaw was exactly right for the role and the pilot film *Regan*, made at a cost of £85,000 with John in the title role, introduced Detective Inspector Jack Regan as a hard-working, hard-drinking, impatient and often frustrated policeman.

His wife, played by Janet Key, had left him after years of coming second to her husband's pursuit of villains and he had a younger sidekick, Sergeant Carter, on his crime-busting adventures, played by Dennis Waterman.

Thaw and Waterman had met long before, when Dennis was sixteen and in his last year at drama school. John was filming for a TV play near Regent's Park and every lunchtime he would take a boat out on the canal for some peace and quiet. One day Dennis asked if he could accompany him and he spent the entire time picking John's brain about the world of acting. John was impressed with Dennis's enthusiastic attitude, even if it had disturbed his normally tranquil lunchbreak.

The *Regan* pilot film screened on 4 June 1974 was well received. It made number three in the television ratings with an audience of 7 million, a decent enough figure for Ted Childs, who had produced *Regan*, to begin developing a series of thirteen one-hour programmes with Kennedy-Martin.

The partnership between John Thaw and Dennis Waterman was generally agreed to have gelled on screen and to have proved harmonious off it, and the two actors were signed up for the series, which was to be called *The Sweeney*.

The title was derived from Sweeney Todd, Cockney rhyming slang for the Flying Squad. It was a vernacular term much used by both criminals and the police since the Flying Squad was first formed in the 1920s to combat criminals with cars. The term Flying Squad had been coined after the special police unit was equipped with a fleet of sports cars linked by radio.

As in the pilot, Regan was to be the main character in *The Sweeney* and Ted Childs, in his format for the show, largely written as a brief to his writers, fleshed out Regan's background and character. He was thirty-six, a tough, resourceful detective who had been in the Flying Squad for four years, Childs explained. He was the total professional, a twenty-four-hour-a-day cop whose commitment to his career had led to the break-up of his marriage. He was now divorced but regularly visited his eight-year-old daughter. He was prone to casualness with women, but not promiscuity. Regan was also contemptuous of the bureaucracy which characterized much of the police service, and his casual style of dressing was one of his methods of showing this resentment. His philosophy was: 'Don't bother me with forms and procedures, let me get out there and nick villains.'

A successful detective, Regan was very much his own man and he would sometimes pursue criminals with a degree of ruthlessness which could shock people used to seeing him as a cynically humorous but compassionate human being.

For John Thaw, the role presented a thrilling and stimulating challenge. He knew the part could turn him into a major star. 'The great thing about the Flying Squad is that it gets in almost everywhere where serious crime is concerned. It offers unlimited plots,' he enthused. 'I see Regan as a cop who is finely balanced between crime and the law. If he wasn't a very good cop he would be a very good crook. I know a few policemen and they have got to be as cunning as the villains. We want to add depth to the usual police thriller. The police are real people, too, after all. There's a lot of frustration in their job.'

Like Regan, John was from Manchester, divorced and had known the pain of being a loving father to a daughter from a marriage that had failed to last. But there any resemblance to Regan abruptly ended. 'In real life I'm not nearly as tough as Regan,' said John. 'But basically we're both pretty down-to-earth blokes. So from that point of view it was good casting.'

Paired with John was Dennis Waterman as his subordinate Sergeant George Carter, a sharp, tough, twenty-six-year-old Cockney who admired Regan and enjoyed working with him even if they frequently argued over style of working. He always called his more volatile superior 'Guv'. Regan and Carter's main concern was major crime, which frequently meant robbery of one sort or another.

A third running character was Detective Chief Inspector Frank Haskins, played by Garfield Morgan, who believed the rulebook was there to be strictly observed not ignored or torn to shreds – as was frequently the case where Regan and Carter were concerned.

When Scotland Yard heard what *The Sweeney* was all about they offered to provide an adviser, and former Flying Squad detective John Quarrie was assigned to oversee the production on police procedures. Quarrie's appointment had a double benefit. It meant viewers were assured of authenticity on police practice and deskwork but they also automatically assumed that Regan's womanizing, drinking and penchant for delivering an occasional violent 'knuckle sandwich' must be true to life, too.

Even though he was sometimes working sixteen-hour days, six days a week, John threw himself into the role with tireless energy and conviction and with a force which gave the character of Regan great depth. He won glowing reviews from the critics, especially for the way he consistently conveyed Regan's bitter and world-weary view of the dirty job he had to do.

'I sometimes hate this bastard place,' a despairing Regan once raged. 'It's a bloody holiday camp for thieves and weirdos . . . all the rubbish. You age prematurely trying to sort some of them out. You try and protect the public and all they do is call you fascist. You nail a villain and some ponced-up, pin-striped amateur barrister screws you up like an old fag packet on a point of procedure, then pops off for a game of squash and a glass of Madeira. He's taking home thirty grand a year and we can just about afford ten days in Eastbourne and a second-hand car.'

Often the racy, hard-hitting action was topped off with a quirky, sly and earthy humour. 'We're the Sweeney, son, and we ain't had our dinner yet,' Regan menacingly told one suspect. And asked if he drank on duty, Regan replied 'Only whisky.' Introducing Carter to a colleague, Regan remarked: 'This is my sergeant. He hits people.' The action was also spiced with occasional funny moments, including one risqué scene with a girl whom Regan had persuaded to sleep with him while she wore nothing except a German helmet.

Devotees of *The Sweeney* also had to become familiar with a whole new vocabulary, as Regan and Carter mixed with London's low life to build up contacts in the criminal fraternity. Armed robbers were 'blaggers', cash was 'readies' and an informant was a 'snout'. And there were special lines of dialogue that the writers would try to include, of which the favourite was 'Get yer trousers on. You're nicked,' usually directed at some slumbering suspect as the duo muscled their way through a front door in a dawn raid. The London-flavoured dialogue was convincing enough for John to be regularly asked which part of the capital he hailed from. 'Manchester' was the answer which surprised many.

Thaw and Waterman were contrasting figures, John with his already markedly greying hair and Dennis tall, lean, fair-haired with virile good looks. They did many of their own stunts and as a double act on screen in their fashionable flared trousers, kipper ties and bomber jackets, they were a dynamic duo who complemented each other, especially in the later episodes when Carter's wife, played by Stephanie Turner, had died. That gave Regan and Carter the chance to share more time together eyeing up the birds, supporting each other when their relationships inevitably foundered, and studying life through a beer glass together. 'I was very lucky in *The Sweeney* to strike up a great partnership with Dennis Waterman,' said John. 'We got on very well together and I think it showed on screen.'

Dennis was an extrovert while John was naturally shy but, although very different, the two men had plenty in common. Like John, Dennis had been through one marriage and, like John, he had also enjoyed a healthy TV career. Waterman had been to stage school and had first made a good impression in *Just William* and then in the film *Up the Junction*.

During filming of *The Sweeney*, John found Dennis's cheerful attitude to work infectious. John had always taken his work extremely seriously and as a disciplined actor he was regarded as a consummate professional. But on *The Sweeney* Waterman taught him how to relax more and find humour in his work. 'I can have a joke during work now as well as afterwards which I've never been able to do before,' said John. For his part, John boosted Dennis's self-confidence. 'Through John's discipline and strength, I have learned to calm down and be more in control,' he said.

That wonderful screen partnership blossomed into a

Above: John (front row, far left) in short trousers at his Uncle Albert's wedding.

Left: John's mother, Dolly.

Below: A star is born: John's birth certificate.

CERTIFIED COPY OF AN ENTRY OF BIRTH

GIVEN AT THE GENERAL REGISTER OFFICE

Application Number: B 013126/A

REGISTRATION DISTRICT Manchester

1942 BIRTH in the Sub-district of Manchester Eastern in the County Borough of Manchester

Columns:	1.	2.	3.	4.	5.	6.	7.	8.	9.	10*
No.	When and where born	Name, if any	Sex	Name and surname of father	Name, surname and maiden surname of mother	Occupation of father	Signature, description and residence of informant	When registered	Signature of registrar	Name entered after registration
173	Third January 1942 9 Harpurhey Grove Longsight	John Edward	Boy	John Edward Thaw	Dorothy Thaw formerly Abbott	Tool Setter Aircraft works	J.E. Thaw Father Stowell Street West Gorton	Fifth January 1942	Warwick	

CERTIFIED to be a true copy of an entry in the certified copy of a Register of Births in the District above mentioned.

Given at the GENERAL REGISTER OFFICE, under the Seal of the said Office, the 10th day of March 1998

BXBY 415492

CAUTION:- It is an offence to falsify a certificate or to make or knowingly use a false certificate or a copy of a false certificate intending it to be accepted as genuine to the prejudice of any person or to possess a certificate knowing it to be false without lawful authority.

WARNING: THIS CERTIFICATE IS NOT EVIDENCE OF THE IDENTITY OF THE PERSON PRESENTING IT.

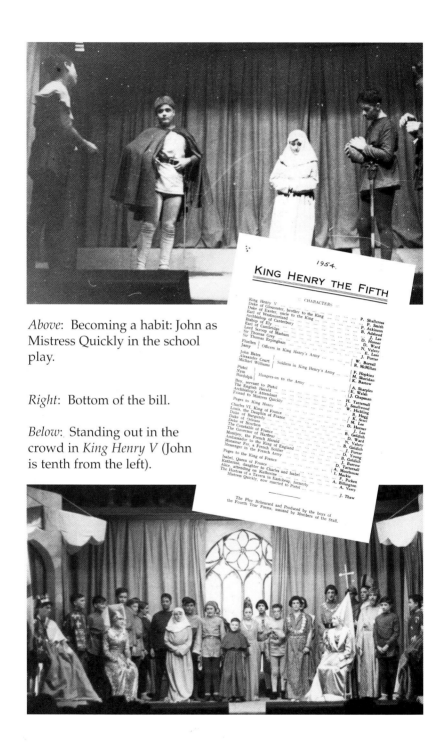

Above: Becoming a habit: John as Mistress Quickly in the school play.

Right: Bottom of the bill.

Below: Standing out in the crowd in *King Henry V* (John is tenth from the left).

1954.

KING HENRY THE FIFTH

:: CHARACTERS ::

King Henry V	P. Shallcross
Duke of Gloucester, brother to the King	P. Smith
Duke of Exeter, uncle to the King	P. Atkinson
Earl of Westmoreland	B. Adahead
Archbishop of Canterbury	A. Lee
Bishop of Ely	D. Horner
Earl of Cambridge	D. Ward
Lord Scroop of Masham	N. Valery
Sir Thomas Grey	E. Lees
Sir Thomas Erpingham	J. Porter
Fluellen	W. Borrell
Jamy } Officers in King Henry's Army	R. McMillan
John Bates	P. Hopkins
Alexander Court } Soldiers in King Henry's Army	M. Shotow
Michael Williams	K. Bastow
Pistol	A. Sharples
Nym	E. Walsh
Bardolph } Hangers-on to the Army	J. Chapman
Boy, servant to Pistol	H. Tattersall
The English Herald	J. Smallwood
Archbishop's Attendant	W. Hickling
Friend to Mistress Quickly	R. Hogg
Pages to King Henry	K. Sniel
	M. Lee
Charles VI, King of France	D. Horner
Louis, the Dauphin of France	J. Lee
Duke of Burgundy	B. Goldich
Duke of Orleans	D. Ward
Duke of Bourbon	N. Valery
The Constable of France	B. Goldich
The Governor of Harfleur	D. Porter
Montjoy, the French Herald	B. Young
Ambassador to the King of England	B. Goldich
Monsieur Fer, a French Soldier	J. Barrow
Messenger to the French Army	D. Tattersall
Pages to the King of France	A. Moorhouse
Isabel, Queen of France	L. Mackie
Katharine, daughter to Charles and Isabel	F. Picken
Alice, attending on Katherine	A. Billington
The Hostess of a Tavern in Eastcheap, formerly Mistress Quickly, now married to Pistol	A. Vesty
	J. Thaw

The Play Rehearsed and Produced by the boys of the Fourth Year Forms, assisted by Members of the Staff.

Above:
Schooldays: John with school pals Harvey Bryant (left)
and Graham Rothwell (centre).

Right: John as Sir Toby Belch with Gemma Jones in *Twelfth Night*, at Stratford.

Below: On his way to TV fame in *The Passengers*.

Above: The start of a dynamic partnership: John Thaw and Dennis Waterman in the TV film *Regan*. (Scope Features)

Right: John's first TV starring role in *Redcap*. (Scope Features)

Below: John with Bob Hoskins and Pam Ashton in *Thick as Thieves*. (Scope Features)

Top left: John with his *Sweeney* co-star, Dennis Waterman. (Rex Features)

Inset left: Combing for clues: John as Inspector Jack Regan. (Rex Features)

Bottom left: Inspector Regan taking time out with his family. (Transworld Feature Syndicate)

Above: 'Get your trousers on, you're nicked!' An arresting moment for Regan and Carter. (Scope Features)

Right: *Sweeney* action: Regan and Carter after villains on the run. (Scope Features)

Left:
Portrait of a star.
(All Action)

Right: A new door
opened for John in
Absence of War.
(All Action)

lasting friendship and Thaw's popular co-star will always be grateful. Dennis said: 'When the series started in 1975 I was just one of the coppers in the squad. But John kept pushing me into more things. He'd say, "Give this scene to Dennis. Do a close-up." It was his idea to develop us as a sort of double act. He could have grabbed all the action for himself.'

Action was the key word in *The Sweeney*, both on screen and off. Filming moved at incredible speed, with each £40,000 film shot over ten days, which realized an average of five minutes' edited screen time per day. The film unit was ready to move quickly to and from locations which were rarely more than one hour away from the main set based at Colet Court, an old school building in Hammersmith in west London, which served as Regan and Carter's Flying Squad office.

The Sweeney frequently came under fire for its violent content and its foul language, as Thames TV feared it would. The Thames hierarchy was so nervous of negative reactions from the press about the levels of violence that a not quite so rough and tough episode called 'Thin Ice' was shown to Fleet Street's television correspondents as a preview, rather than the opening episode called 'Ringer'.

The Thames executives did not have long to wait before the protests began. Several of Britain's high-ranking policemen did not approve of the image it gave of the police, and Sir David McNee, the Metropolitan Police Commissioner, criticized *The Sweeney*'s possible influence on young officers, saying: 'For a policeman to carry out police duties by following *The Sweeney* would be the road to disaster.'

Inevitably John found himself having to defend the show and he spoke out on several occasions, declaring how much he detested violence. 'I hate it,' he said. 'I believe there is no gratuitous violence in the series. What there is comes out of the situations. After all, we are trying to get some feeling of realism. By the nature of their job, Flying Squad boys have got to be tough. Regan never gets aggressive with anyone who doesn't deserve it.

'I enjoy playing Regan, but I don't like him. I don't like his hardness or his lack of sensitivity to other people's feelings. But what *The Sweeney* has made me realize is what a rotten job it is. Hard, often unpleasant work, terrible hours and then they get abuse poured on them by everyone who's ever been nicked for speeding or for parking on a yellow line. I wouldn't do it at any price.'

So convincing was John as Regan that Sheila had to explain occasionally that, despite the Regan image, her husband was nothing like him at home. 'He frightens me sometimes when I watch him on the box,' she said. 'He looks so aggressive but he's really a bit of a softie. He works so hard getting bruised and battered that it's a pale shadow of a man who comes home – not exactly a roaring lion bashing down the door.'

John's following grew but he went through a phase of hating the tag Jack Regan, mainly because of what he termed 'nuisance value'. He would find complete strangers winding down their car windows to mutter something about Regan to him and he was recognized and pointed at wherever he went. One day he discovered a young girl camped outside his home in Chiswick. A devoted fan, she had arrived from Nottingham with a friend in the hope of catching a glimpse of her idol. John had no idea she was there until she knocked on his door at seven in the morning. Gallantly he invited her in and made her a cup of coffee to warm her up. She later went on her way, delighted at having met John Thaw, and took it upon herself to start circulating news to other fans about what he was up to.

As the series progressed controversy was never far away and criticism came from all quarters. Mary Whitehouse and her National Viewers' and Listeners' Association deploring the bad language, the sex and violence was predictable enough. 'Police officers are not as a matter of course foul-mouthed, sadistically violent and promiscuous,' Mary protested. The NVLA even counted thirty-seven incidents of 'foul or coarse' expressions in one episode. Less expected, however, was an assault on the programme from a survey of London boys by Dr William Belson, which suggested that boys exposed to high levels of TV violence as in *The Sweeney* were more likely to commit serious crimes. Ted Childs moved swiftly to counter that allegation by pointing out that many of the show's fans were over sixty. 'If our critics had been right,' he said, 'shopping precincts would have been full of marauding OAPs beating the rest of us over our heads with pension books.'

Then Chief Inspector John Robinson, who lectured on the techniques of catching criminals at the Police Training School, Hendon, publicly complained that each episode of *The Sweeney* gave away too much secret information about police methods. He said of John Thaw's Regan: 'He hands out trade secrets like they were on special offer at a supermarket. Crime is a costly business, not a game, yet here is a programme handing out secrets absolutely free of charge. I don't think there is a young copper who could not learn a thing or two from watching the programme. So you can imagine what it does for the villains. They must welcome it with open arms.'

Former Flying Squad boss Frank Davies also joined in the attack on the show. '*The Sweeney* is an insult to a small group of devoted police officers renowned throughout the world. No policeman keeping observation during a bank raid would spend his time jumping in and out of a woman's bed. As to the violence, senseless shootings and a far-fetched scene depicting an officially approved kidnapping, all this is fantasy.

'The sex scenes worry wives and girlfriends of serving officers. They give a false image of life in the Squad. Neighbours and friends may think it's true.' Davies finished his tirade by suggesting there should be a preface to the series making it clear that it was fiction.

The furore, of course, was not unexpected, but right from the outset Ted Childs had laid down the guidelines and parameters for *The Sweeney*. He wanted to make exciting, action-packed television but he was always aware of his responsibility not to transgress the rules of the Independent Broadcasting Authority (IBA). 'Major crime is very often violent,' he stressed to his team in his format outline, 'and one does not wish to flinch from the reality of this. Nonetheless, the series is being produced for transmission in both afternoon and evening family viewing hours. Accordingly, we must respect the rules laid down by the IBA in respect of language and the detailed description of pathological forms of behaviour. Four-letter words are not permissible, nor can we indulge in 'souped-up' horror, e.g. represent, in slow motion, a security guard having his head blown off by a shotgun.'

Childs was equally clear in his guidelines about action. 'We are not in the "Bondiana" league,' he briefed his team. 'We can cope with a limited number of fight scenes, car chases, shoot-outs, etc. We cannot blow up Jablite representations of St Paul's nor bring the whole of Oxford Street to a grinding halt in order to wreck three police cars inside Selfridge's front window!'

Not everyone was alarmed by *The Sweeney*. Several detectives privately let it be known to Thames TV that they were not too upset at being portrayed as tough and uncompromising, and Battersea detectives presented John Thaw with a silver cigarette box with the engraving: 'We wish all DIs were like you.'

Crucially for Thames TV, Euston Films and John Thaw, the public loved the show – and the format so carefully laid down by Ted Childs. He had each episode opening with a teaser of around three minutes, followed by the opening titles, and the story then played out in three acts. The teaser was usually packed with action – a shooting, a punch-up, skidding cars, squealing brakes, designed to hook viewers from the start with a fast-moving montage of exciting images. It was precision programming and both viewers and advertisers knew what to expect each week. Once they were familiar with the structure and its two leading men, they wanted more of the same with, of course, different stories and different villains.

The writers were given up to a month to write each script, but the hectic pace of the production required them to deliver as quickly as possible. One was written in just three days. The brief to the writers was that John Thaw as Regan should appear in every episode and Dennis Waterman as Carter in approximately ten of the thirteen episodes. In addition to these main characters, there was to be room for three other major speaking roles and up to ten minor speaking parts.

The scripts for *The Sweeney* proved to be consistently good and the production team successfully achieved their goal of injecting the series with a flavour of *The French Connection*, the Hollywood cops and robbers movie which had proved such a huge box-office success. Filmed in semi-documentary style and shot almost entirely in and around Manhattan, *The French Connection* starred Gene Hackman and Roy Scheider as two tough New York cops. Both critics and public found their performances so convincing and natural that some even wondered whether the dialogue had been ad-libbed rather than scripted.

That film's influence on *The Sweeney* was considerable. One scene in *The French Connection* memorably had Gene Hackman as Jimmy 'Popeye' Doyle miserably sipping a drink from a paper cup in a New York street, while keeping a watch on two drug peddlers across the road enjoying a slap-up meal in a Manhattan restaurant. That was the kind of realism to strive for, the production team reminded each other.

The first series of *The Sweeney* made a huge impact. Scheduled on Thursday nights at nine o'clock as an alternative to the news on BBC1, it quickly built up a massive following, with episode eight achieving the highest audience of the first series, pulling in 8.75 million viewers which took it to number two in the ratings. The timing had proved just right.

Buoyed by such instant success, a second series was rapidly put into production and screened in prime time on Monday nights on ITV, just five months after the first series had finished. The second batch of thirteen programmes proved even more of a success than the first.

Episodes six and seven took John Thaw to the top of the TV ratings for the first time and average audiences were well over 8 million again. Dutifully following the show-business premise that a successful idea should be squeezed till the pips squeak, Euston Films took the decision to produce a *Sweeney* feature film for the cinema.

Thames TV put up most of the £1.4 million budget and sought the remainder from EMI. Nat Cohen, then the boss of EMI, made it plain he was an admirer of *The Sweeney*, but before he bankrolled it he naturally wanted to know what extra ingredients a *Sweeney* film would contain to persuade fans of the show to go out on a wet wintry night and spend a few pounds at the cinema. Ted Childs remembers he had no answer to that but he did have a gut feeling it would work, and Cohen had enough faith in him to back the project.

Nevertheless, when EMI came in, everyone was under pressure to make a film that people would pay to see not just in Britain but overseas. The TV show was by now an international success story and went on to be screened in forty different countries ranging from Peru to Swaziland, as well as Spain, Argentina and the major markets of the United States, Australia and Canada. In Canada the director of programmes for channel CTV was actually asked by several viewers to provide subtitles for the Cockney rhyming slang. People complained they could not understand the language of the criminal underworld which peppered the shows.

Quite apart from their financial contribution, EMI's willingness to become a partner in the film was crucial when it came to distribution, for this meant that it would be assured of a UK release through the chain of ABC cinemas owned by EMI.

With David Wickes as director, *Sweeney!* was shot on location in London over a period of five weeks during the spring of 1976. The film, which featured Regan and Carter investigating a suicide and uncovering an elaborate political blackmail scheme, was released in Britain after the second TV series had finished. Loyal fans of the show duly turned the film into a box-office success and it was also sold overseas, including, surprisingly, to China – the first Western film to be shown to the Chinese. A sequel, *Sweeney 2*, soon went into production, with several familiar TV faces like Barry Foster, Ian Bannen, Colin Welland and Diane Keen brought in to add impetus.

By the end of the third TV series, John was feeling jaded and he felt he could get little more out of Regan. Dennis Waterman felt the same way and the two stars gathered everyone together to have a rethink. John suggested that they should all try to treat the fourth series as if it were the first and they threw themselves into it with renewed vigour.

Nevertheless, both John and Dennis now knew it was to be the end of the road for *The Sweeney*. Despite pleas from Thames TV, who envisioned the series continuing for at least another two years, they both wanted to quit while they were ahead. The news broke that they were calling it a day after series four while John was filming on location in Kilburn. 'I was frightened of going stale,' he explained. 'The series started out marvellously and this latest batch is among the best we've ever done. But we want to quit while we are winning.'

It was a brave decision. John later confessed that the price he and Dennis Waterman were paying for the success of *The Sweeney* was just too high. It was affecting their family lives. The long-running series certainly became a strain on life at home. Thaw observed wryly to a friend: 'I'm like a real-life policeman, never knowing what time I am going to get in. And when you are in, you are too tired to be good company.' To make matters worse at home

Sheila was appearing in the West End hit *Annie,* which meant they became like ships that passed in the night.

A gruelling schedule required John to leave home at six in the morning and sometimes he would not return until ten at night. 'Domestically it created a lot of problems for us both,' John explained. 'You'd leave the house at the crack of dawn not knowing what time you'd get back. Occasionally I'd pass Sheila on the stairs and that might be the sum total of our contact in a week. Since we went on filming for six months at a time, I decided enough was enough. I knew I had to get my priorities right.'

Waterman agreed. 'As actors you just can't go on doing the same thing year after year,' he said. 'We're going to miss each other. John and I have had a tremendous working relationship ever since we first started and we've been personal friends off the screen too.'

There was much mourning by loyal fans of *The Sweeney* as Christmas 1978 approached. The fourth batch of thirteen programmes had delivered remarkable audiences for Thames TV. Even the lowest audience figure was nearly 11 million and an incredible 19.05 million viewers tuned in four days before Christmas to watch the penultimate episode of the fourth and final series. This was a remarkable viewing figure, considering the episode in question, called 'Selected Target', was a repeat from series three.

In November avid fans of the show had even seen Eric Morecambe and Ernie Wise, television's most outstanding comedy double act of their generation, making guest appearances in a *Sweeney* episode called 'Hearts and Minds', playing themselves. They were innocent bystanders caught up in a story about a missing professor. Eric and Ern, as they were affectionately known to their adoring public, had invited John Thaw and Dennis

Waterman on to their Christmas TV show two years previously. An invitation to make a guest appearance with the funniest TV double act Britain had ever produced was widely regarded in the acting world, not least by Glenda Jackson and Diana Rigg, as a true accolade and John and Dennis were thrilled to get the call. But, the two actors agreed, on the condition Morecambe and Wise returned the compliment and took roles in their show.

The final episode, called 'Jack or Knave' and written by producer Ted Childs, was screened on 28 December 1978, just a few days before John's thirty-seventh birthday. It began with a bloody and brutal robbery, then, despite a judge's commendation, Regan found himself arrested on suspicion of taking bribes while a detective sergeant back in 1968. He was unceremoniously thrown in a cell like a common felon before being cleared. He emerged, not unnaturally, extremely bitter, allowing John Thaw to bow out as compulsively watchable as when Regan had first arrived on screen two films and fifty-three episodes before.

'I am utterly pissed off with this little lot,' John was able to exit with Regan's customary snarl. 'I've given the best years of my life to this job. I've got eighteen commendations and how does this wonderful police force show its gratitude for all my years of unstinting effort? It bangs me up in a cruddy little cell. I'm going to have to be reinstated and what do you bunch of gleaming, double-eyed hookheads do now? You want me to crawl back to work and be very grateful that I didn't get nicked for something I didn't do. Well you can stuff it.' And with that, Regan and *The Sweeney* vanished from the screen.

The ending did at least leave open the possibility of Regan and Carter returning to their beat at some point in the future if John and Dennis so desired. At periodic intervals over the next five years John received an invitation to lunch with the producers of *The Sweeney*. Ever hopeful of reviving the show, they wanted to sound out John as to whether he ever saw himself returning to the role of Jack Regan. But, proud as he was of *The Sweeney*, John always made it clear he had moved on. Some five years later, however, John did change his mind and he informed the producers he might consider a return.

He had been swayed by a top-ranking police officer asking him when *The Sweeney* would be coming back. He told John how much he and so many others had enjoyed it, adding that since John was an actor, why didn't he give the public what they wanted since it was they who paid his wages?

John went home that night and found it difficult to sleep, his mind buzzing with all the reasons why he'd said he wouldn't step into Regan's shoes again. 'I realized that there was no reason in the world why I shouldn't,' he said. 'I could do a film rather than a series. It would only be six weeks out of my life.'

John had taken the trouble to check with Dennis that he would be agreeable to teaming up again and they decided that although a new TV series was out of the question, Regan and Carter could conceivably return in a film. 'Talking to that policeman reminded me that, dare I say it, *The Sweeney* was a well-made product,' said John. 'It had an appearance of reality, and people seemed to enjoy it.' But the reunion of Regan and Carter never materialized, for both John Thaw and Dennis Waterman were busy with other projects.

John was none too pleased, however, when in 1991 Thames TV revealed plans to repeat *Regan*, the original TV film which spawned *The Sweeney*, just as John was launching his new TV project *Stanley and the Women*. John had given Thames his permission to screen some episodes of *The Sweeney* the previous year, but he felt this was a blatant attempt by Thames to cash in on the film before the company lost its ITV franchise. He branded the decision a disgrace. 'They should be making new shows,' he said, 'not putting out a seventeen-year-old series which will cost them just a few hundred pounds to show.'

The importance of *The Sweeney*'s place in the history of popular drama on British television should not be under-estimated. Indeed, no less a revered media figure than Jeremy Isaacs considered *The Sweeney* 'one of the most successful series ever done for British television'. It took on Hollywood at its own game, played to win, and triumphed. *The Sweeney* overtook the much-heralded American cop series imports *Kojak* and *Starsky and Hutch* and also saw off the BBC's pale imitation *Target*. It provided ITV with a cast-iron peak-time ratings winner, and became a much admired model for the next generation of programme-makers.

John Thaw's contribution to the success of the show was immense. Indisputably he made Regan *the* TV cop of the Seventies, with his forceful portrayal which had that price-less asset of appealing to both men and women.

Today John Thaw's television techniques are much admired by his fellow actors and it was while filming *The Sweeney* that he quickly found out the dos and don'ts of props and the problems they can cause with continuity. 'I learned them on *The Sweeney*,' said John. 'Don't smoke in a scene if you can help it, for example. Hold the thing but don't smoke it. If you have to do six or seven takes you'll end up green in the face. Later, when I played Morse, who drank gallons of real ale, that became vital. Luckily I don't like beer. But anyway, you must just take the pint glass, take a sip and put it down. Don't touch it again, it makes life so much easier!'

The Sweeney remained in viewers' memories for many years and to such an extent that, twenty years on, Nissan based a multi-million-pound advertising campaign on a clever spoof *Sweeney* advertisement, with a Regan-style cop leaping from his car and bellowing 'Shut it!' to anyone who dared to utter a word.

The advertisement for the Nissan Almera was considered enough of a novelty to be unveiled amid much fanfare at the Prince Charles Theatre in London's West End. The theatre was bathed in flashing blue light and swathed in tape proclaiming 'Police line – do not cross' while two Almeras were rammed, *Sweeney*-style, on to the pavement. Guests at the launch were then invited to soak up the nostalgic atmosphere with the help of 'a four-strong bulging-bellied polyester-shirted formation dance team and an a cappella *Sweeney* theme-tune combo whose choreography is entirely inspired by Flying Squad poses.'

Eventually repeated on satellite TV station UK Gold in the nineties, *The Sweeney* attracted a whole new audience, as well as a hard core of devoted fans, thrilled to have the chance to watch the shows a second time round. It also picked up a younger audience with repeats on Channel 5.

Now *The Sweeney* is set to be remade for TV, masterminded once again by Ian Kennedy-Martin, with Dennis Waterman earmarked for promotion to the senior officer in the Flying Squad but with Regan taking no part, having retired to run a salmon farm in Scotland.

The Sweeney had been John Thaw's life for four years and his career might have taken a very different course if Ted Childs had not offered him the role of Regan the day after he had married Sheila. By that time John was familiar to millions of television viewers from a highly praised situation comedy called *Thick as Thieves*, written for London Weekend Television by Dick Clement and Ian La Frenais.

The show starred Bob Hoskins as Dobbs, a small-time crook who had come out of jail to find his best mate Stan, played by John Thaw, had moved in with his wife Annie, played by Pat Ashton. The six-part series was much acclaimed and the two writers wanted to develop it further, sending both men back to prison.

Although London Weekend liked the idea, they dithered about going ahead because they deemed the writing too clever and felt it might go over the heads of an ITV audience. Their hesitation meant John was free to take up Ted Childs's offer to star in *Regan*. Clement and La Frenais took their idea to the BBC instead and Ronnie Barker's marvellous TV creation of prisoner Norman Stanley Fletcher in *Porridge* was the memorably entertaining outcome.

Once the decision to end *The Sweeney* had been made, John couldn't make a quick enough getaway. Only a week after filming his final scenes as Jack Regan, Thaw was hard at work on a new television role that was as far away from the charismatic copper as possible.

He took on the part of struggling, middle-aged boxing manager Dinny Matthews in a BBC *Play For Today* called *The Sporting Club Dinner*. 'I picked the part because it was as different from Regan as it could be,' said John. 'The first thing I have to do now is to break away from being stuck with the tough copper image.'

With slicked-back grey hair and a worried expression, he instantly left Regan far behind. Matthews was a manager with a burning ambition one day to produce a real champion. But when his best prospect, played by Billy McColl, was offered a vital fight, Matthews was forced to struggle with his conscience, because the young boxer was out of training and in no condition to fight.

For the first few months after filming had finished John had no other work to throw himself into. He was, he says, edgy and couldn't sit still and Sheila began telling him he should get back to work as he was getting under her feet.

6

FAMILY AND WORK

John Thaw simply couldn't bear the front-of-house area at London's National Theatre. It's nothing to do with any of the fine work he had done in the thriving centre of Britain's stage world. It's just that this is where he was surprised in 1981 by Eamon Andrews and the big red book of *This Is Your Life*. For the shy star, the sentimental show was a deeply embarrassing experience.

He could hardly duck out of it as he had taken part enthusiastically in his wife Sheila's own television trip down memory lane some five years before. As the time for the surprise approached Sheila was terrified that her husband would refuse to take part in the programme. For the most part, he sat and squirmed his way through the recording, except when first his father arrived and then, from Australia, his brother Raymond. At that point John Thaw's smile lit up the screen as the two men closest to him were briefly reunited for the watching viewers.

John was grabbed by Eamon on his way out of a back-stage meeting about his starring role in *Sergeant Musgrave's Dance*. He thought he was on his way out to the car park when he was suddenly confronted by a waiting crowd of close friends singing round the piano. Well, not quite all close friends. The actor John Bluthal just happened to be going to a show that night and was dragged in by some of the others for the booze-up. On the show Eamon announced: 'And here are all your very good friends – Tony Selby, Dennis Waterman, Ian Hendry, James Ellis . . .' Sheila laughed afterwards that 'on the video recording we have, John Bluthal – whom John had never met in his life – is clearly heard to mutter as he shakes John's hand, "Sorry about this mate." '

The screening was one of the most popular *This Is Your Life* programmes ever made and at his home in Poynton on the outskirts of Manchester, Harvey Bryant raised a glass of champagne to his old friend's prediction 'One day I'll be on *This Is Your Life*' coming true. Ironically, when it happened, the evening was one of the most excruciating of Thaw's life.

In 1979, after *The Sweeney* and the boxing drama, which brought the usual highly professional performance from Thaw, he was even more pleased by another job offer. 'I had decided to give up television for a while: it's like the old music hall, you can be good but if you stay on too long you're rotten. Then, out of the blue, came this call from my agent saying there was a new Tom Stoppard play on offer and would I like to read it? You don't say "No" to that kind of question, particularly if you're an actor who has just turned down *Whose Life is it Anyway?* and is still kicking himself whenever he thinks about it.'

The Tom Stoppard play was *Night and Day*, and Thaw gave a brilliant portrayal of hard-bitten Australian journalist Dick Wagner which gave him just the break he wanted from the small screen. Yet he was quick to point out that without the success of *The Sweeney* he would never have been offered the part.

The West End hit opened in Wimbledon, where the production was struck by some first-night catastrophes. Co-star Diana Rigg said: 'The revolve went round the wrong way and there was an awful splintering of furniture. There was a little boy in the class who got his lines all wrong and I tried to save the day but I was not familiar enough with the script and I fed John with a line that was five pages later. John and I looked at each other and we just started to laugh. Then the audience started to laugh, thank God. They got the joke and we just went back to the beginning and started again.' The two stars remained friends and Diana noted afterwards that 'During eight months you get to know somebody terribly well. And I think John is a marvellous actor and, more importantly, a very dear man.'

John said: 'Television makes you a star and I'd never underrate it, nor do I go along with the old actors' theory that it's a second-class kind of life.' In 1983 he spent a year with the Royal Shakespeare Company at Stratford-upon-Avon. He alternated in three plays which included appearing as Cardinal Wolsey in *Henry VIII*, as Sir Toby Belch in *Twelfth Night* and as Nick in *The Time of Your Life*. John was deeply moved by the reception he inspired from people more used to watching him on television than on stage. 'I've had letters, lovely letters from people who have been to Stratford and written saying they didn't think I would be able to do it,' said John. 'They're not being rude, it's because they only know me from *The Sweeney*, so they think, "Good Lord, I didn't know he could play a cardinal."'

Like most actors, John Thaw appreciates playing to a live audience, but the grind of a long theatrical run does not appeal to him. 'My problem with the theatre', he said, 'is that the gilt wears off pretty soon. What starts off as exciting, with the adrenalin pumping, becomes a bit of a chore after a few weeks. Television is a more inward type of acting. You rely more on yourself. It's between you and the camera. Some actors asked to do *Morse*, with its rigorous schedule, might find it as mind-boggling as I think it would be to do *Hamlet* twice a day.'

John had appeared in films early in his acting career, with the part in *The Loneliness of the Long Distance Runner*, and in 1968 he had a role in an absorbing military movie, *The Bofors Gun*. This was set in a British barracks in Germany in the mid-1950s and starred his great friend Nicol Williamson as an embittered Irish rebel.

Perhaps it is understandable that John achieved his greatest success on the small screen after his view of film-making was jaundiced by his experiences on the film *The Grass is Singing*. Even in the fairytale world of movie-making, it's hard to produce a masterpiece of cinema when the film crew are chased by enraged elephants, the director falls for his leading lady, the producer is shot at by bandits, a film unit just manages to escape with their lives after an ambush, much of the wardrobe is stolen a few days before the cameras start rolling and there are frequent arguments over the script.

The situation became harder still when, in addition to these difficulties, several of the crew fall ill, a key actor comes close to death after an eye injury haemorrhages, a cameraman suffers concussion when he falls out of a tree, another goes into shock after finding himself suddenly cornered by a spitting cobra, and the frailties of human flesh are cruelly exposed on sixteen-hour working days by a fiercely unforgiving African sun by day, and equally unrelenting biting insects by night.

It was no surprise, therefore, that John Thaw had a withering comment to make when asked about his experience of filming *The Grass is Singing* out in the Zambian bush for three months. 'It was pure hell,' he said. Ironically, however, he was subsequently to earn perhaps one of the best reviews of his life as a movie actor when the film was released in Britain.

It was easy to see why a starring role opposite an acclaimed Hollywood actress in a film based on a Doris Lessing best-seller must originally have sounded so appealing to John. *The Grass is Singing* is a searing saga of how Mary Turner, a white South African woman, marries a well-meaning but failing farmer. As her marriage and life disintegrate and she descends into poverty, she goes mad under the stress. She comes to be dependent upon a servant, Moses, whom she once regularly abused, and is eventually killed by him.

John was cast as the woman's luckless husband Dick Turner, and he immediately recognized the role as an opportunity to play a thoroughly complex character. Dick Turner may be one of life's losers but while everything he touches turns to disaster he evokes sympathy for the way he tries to be a decent husband and a good farmer and employer.

After talk of Janet Suzman or Glenda Jackson playing Mary, the leading role went to Karen Black, a Hollywood star with a reputation for being a versatile and accomplished actress with a rare on-screen sensuality. By co-starring opposite Karen, clearly *The Grass is Singing* was a chance for John's stature as an actor to rise to a higher level.

When Black came to *The Grass is Singing*, there was no doubting her pedigree. She had turned to acting by attending Lee Strasberg's famous Actors' Studio in New York while she was working as a waitress. The Studio had groomed many for stardom, including Marilyn Monroe, but on leaving Black found herself toiling in minor stage roles before eventually landing a part in the Broadway production of *The Playroom* in 1965.

Critically acclaimed for her stage work, she then headed west, making her debut on screen in 1967 in *You're a Big Boy Now* before raising eyebrows as a drugged-out prostitute in the 1969 smash *Easy Rider*, with Jack Nicholson and Peter Fonda. The following year Black earned an Oscar nomination for her supporting performance as a working-class waitress in *Five Easy Pieces*.

She went on to become one of the most prolific screen stars of the seventies, with starring roles in major movies like *The Great Gatsby*, *The Day of the Locust* and as a country music star in *Nashville*. So by the time she arrived in Zambia there was no doubting her versatility. She had enjoyed some of her greatest successes in character roles that made use of her offbeat, squint-eyed looks and her chameleonic talents.

Completing the line-up of key characters as Moses was black South African actor John Kani, who had been imprisoned for his opposition to apartheid. He had also won a name for himself and a prestigious Tony Award for his stage performance in the Athol Fugard anti-apartheid play *Sizwe Bansi is Dead*, which had toured the world.

At the helm of the movie was largely unknown director Michael Raeburn, who had grown up in Rhodesia. He had harboured a deep passion for the film project ever since being profoundly moved by Doris Lessing's book. Raeburn battled to have the film made in Africa after the BBC had expressed an interest in filming it in a studio and the Hollywood moguls had indicated they would prefer to film in Yugoslavia.

Raeburn's persistence paid off and, with Doris Lessing's blessing, he persuaded the Swedish Film Institute and a Zambian consortium to bankroll the film to the tune of around $3 million. But the omens were not good when Raeburn was hospitalized with a heart infection just weeks before shooting was due to begin. John and other members of the cast and crew could not help but notice that Raeburn looked anything but in full bloom of health as filming began. Karen Black, however, was soon looking at him in a very different light – Raeburn promptly fell in love with her.

It was little wonder that visitors to the set at Zambia's Kafue Game Reserve could feel all manner of tensions in the air. A fragile frostiness had developed between John and Karen Black. At one point he chose to have very little to do with her except when called upon to film their scenes.

A clash between the two stars in a movie is not uncommon but the iciness between John and Karen was compounded by a sudden script change which incorporated the sad heroine being ravished by Moses. This new twist put a very different complexion on the film and both John Thaw and John Kani, not to mention the African backers, were none too pleased about this injection of sexual and racial tension. 'All this nonsense about sex is totally gratuitous, a perversion of the book,' John angrily told one visitor to the set, while Kani insisted he would not relish raping anybody and resented Doris Lessing's story being turned into 'bedroom drama'. Increasingly, Raeburn and Black, who supported his rewrites, became more and more isolated as they stuck out for the new scenes to be included.

The rewrites included two rape scenes, and quite apart

from the opposition to them from his two male leads, Raeburn then had to contend with the Swedish Film Institute pointing out that this wasn't the script they had originally enthused over.

With such disharmony all round him, John's thoughts frequently turned to home. Although he was being put up in first-class hotels, including a fabulous suite by the Victoria Falls, he missed Sheila and would eagerly look forward to her letters, which had to be brought out to the set in the bush from the airport more than 200 miles away.

'I got terribly homesick,' he said. 'I was missing home and family and that feeling of security they give you. At one point I nearly ran out on them. I felt I couldn't bear it any more and I thought: "To hell with the consequences, I'm going to get the next plane out!" But there were only three flights a week from Lusaka and I picked the day when there wasn't a plane. So I had to stay another day and by then I'd got over it.

'Strangely enough, the worst times were the odd day off when everybody else had gone off to work and you're sitting in the hotel. In theory it sounds great – relaxing by the pool in the sun, having a drink – but in practice you just go mad because you don't want to be there. It's like being in prison and you get to thinking, "Why am I here?"

'I was going to make another picture after *The Grass is Singing* which meant going abroad, but as a result of my African experience I wouldn't do it.' And John's final verdict on Karen Black was: 'Potty!'

It was inevitable the lack of harmony on set would spill over off-screen. John kept himself to himself and studiously distanced himself from Karen Black. She, anyway, had brought out to the location her five-year-old son Hunter from her marriage to screenwriter Kit Carson and she busied herself playing mother as well as star. For those who were happy to listen, Karen was also ready to expound some of the offbeat Californian platitudes of the day.

Amid all the divisions and the acrimony, one thing everybody agreed upon was that John Thaw was putting in a fine performance. Despite the sweltering 100-degree heat and all the other difficulties surrounding the shooting, John had the admiration of everyone as he went about his work. Even the lowliest aides on the movie would stop whatever they were doing to watch John when it came to filming his scenes.

Dogged by difficulties from the start, the production's final week saw Raeburn collapsing with hepatitis. Nevertheless, he brought the film in on time and it was just as well. When everyone flew out of Lusaka, the distant sound of gunshots could be heard as army rebels attempted a coup.

By the time *The Grass is Singing* was ready for release, the Swedish producers had overruled Raeburn's inclusion of the rape scenes. Film critics generally agreed how difficult it was to bring Doris Lessing's book to the screen, but Margaret Hinxman in the *Daily Mail* was lavish in her praise of John. She wrote: 'Corners are cut to tell the story which begins with the wife's inexplicable murder by a proud black servant and then flashes back to the events that led up to it. By his very presence John Thaw overcomes that deficiency. Through him we come to know this awkward, inarticulate man who was born a loser. You understand the pathetic inadequacy behind his endless crop failures. It's a superb unstinting performance.'

Oscar-winning film director Richard Attenborough is a great believer in John Thaw's acting ability and has twice coaxed him on to the big screen for successful film roles. In the acclaimed and controversial South African movie *Cry Freedom* John was alarmingly menacing as the secret service chief. And Attenborough called again when he was filming *Chaplin* to offer him the role of Fred Karno.

John said: 'Like most actors, Charlie Chaplin meant a lot to me. I remember as a boy going to see him at the Saturday morning pictures at the Odeon in Burnage. And over the years I have seen the classics on television. Films like *The Kid* and *Modern Times* are wonderful. I was pleased the script considered the forces that made him the man he was. The film was certainly no whitewash.'

John Thaw never shied away from controversy and when offered the leading role in a powerful BBC film about uncompromising British wartime leader, Air Marshal Arthur 'Bomber' Harris, he was pleased to accept. Harris was in control of Bomber Command when thousands of Germans were killed towards the end of the war, and afterwards remained fiercely unrepentant about his actions, which were instrumental in the deaths of around 100,000 citizens of Dresden.

Thaw's powerful portrayal brilliantly conveyed Harris's famous ruthless determination, and showed millions of viewers another aspect of the remarkable range of his acting talents. John Thaw said at the time: 'I imagine a guy like Harris wouldn't exactly enjoy destroying a town, but he would enjoy having the authority to say go and destroy it. It is the authorization of the act, the sense of power. He would probably have been a good chairman of a large company.'

It was a widely acclaimed performance, yet playing it tough was no problem to the former *Sweeney* star, who was quick to distance his own personality from that of the fearsome Bomber Harris. 'To be believable, everything an actor does must be in him – otherwise he wouldn't be able to do it. It's just bringing out elements in a part, hoping you don't end up bringing them out too often in your private life.'

In 1981 John presented a ten-part series on child abuse called *When the Bough Breaks*. It was a sensitive BBC2 production that Thaw threw himself fully behind. 'I feel strongly about child abuse,' he said. 'The whole tenor of the programme is to tell parents who hit out that they're not alone. It is a message I wanted to get across to isolated parents.'

In the same year he also starred in a rare costume drama as Sir Francis Drake in an ambitious Westward Television production. John said drily: 'The costume is different but there are similarities between Regan and Drake. Both are independent, tough and stubborn. They decide what they want and they go out and get it. Like Regan, Drake does things I wouldn't dream of doing. For example, a Portuguese prisoner helps Drake but Drake's reward is to drop him in it. In reality Drake was part cop and part robber. He was just this side of being a pirate. He conned his crew rotten and executed one of his best friends when he thought there was going to be a mutiny. What really counted against Drake was that he was of lowly birth. The aristocrats didn't mind him saving Britain from Spain, but they kicked up a right stink when he tried to buy a mansion too close to them!'

Drake sank without trace in the ratings but the career of its star was unaffected. John Thaw was his own severest critic. When he watched any of his work on screen he constantly found moments where he could have been better, which is inclined to spoil the effect of the piece. But when he watched himself in Douglas Livingstone's powerful Northern Ireland film *We'll Support You Ever More* in 1985, he was so swept away by the story he forgot to focus on his own imagined faults. Thaw played Geoff Hollins, a man whose only son David, a second lieutenant in the British Army, was murdered by the IRA while on a secret mission. Two years later when he finds out that a man is to stand trial for the murder, Geoff sets out to discover the truth for himself.

When he sat down at home to watch the play John Thaw found himself deeply moved. And the effect stayed with him for hours afterwards. John recalled: 'Sheila said to me, "What's up with you?" and I said, "It can only be the play." I just couldn't get images from it out of my mind and I can honestly say that has never happened to me before in twenty-five years in this game. There have been plenty of plays about Northern Ireland by Irish writers, but I don't think there has been anything quite like this before, with an ordinary Englishman going to Northern Ireland as a total innocent and investigating for himself what's really going on.'

It was John's first visit to the Province. Sheila had been there with the Royal Shakespeare Company a while back and had told him how kind and giving the people were, so to that extent he was prepared. In other ways it was as much of a revelation to John as it was to Geoff Hollins. He wasn't prepared for the appalling dereliction in some parts of Belfast and the conditions that people had to live in. He thought it was far worse than the worst slums on the mainland. And though he did take an interest in current affairs and read the papers, he did not know there was a Peace Wall in Belfast dividing the Catholic and Protestant communities. As the character says in the play:

'You're always reading about the Berlin Wall, but never about this one.'

The media coverage also left John unprepared for the beauty of the countryside. He said: 'The only time you see it on television is when a patrol has been ambushed in a country lane and then you don't take it in. But if you look past the central court in Belfast you see lovely green hills and just ten minutes' drive from the city centre you're in the most beautiful countryside. Having been there, I have a much better idea about what is going on, but like everyone else I still haven't a clue what the answer is.'

Variety continued to be the spice of life as John Thaw played to great success in the witty comedy series *Home to Roost*. Written by Eric Chappell, then hot from his success with *Duty Free*, the show had Thaw playing a divorced dad struggling to cope with his truculent teenage son, played by Reece Dinsdale.

A superior script had the two stars with a success on their hands, a rare position for anyone in an ITV sitcom, then and now. An example: 'Why did you never hug me when I was little?' demands the boy. 'You were always covered in jam,' responds the father. John enjoyed the change of gear: 'Since I am an actor rather than a comedian I play it for real in *Home to Roost* and it comes out funny. It is the kind of show every parent and teenager can identify with.' And the show gave Sheila Hancock a rare chance to act with her husband when she arrived to guest star as his awkward ex-wife. John says: 'Sheila was worried in case we had a row on the morning we were due to film together. But we made sure we didn't.'

The success of *Home to Roost* pleased John, but playing comedy on televison meant accepting the double challenge of performing to the studio audience as well as the cameras, which has driven many lesser actors to distraction. He felt the pressure but still got wonderful reviews, but he was less impressed when critics hailed him as a new comic talent. 'About ninety per cent of my theatre work over the last twenty-five years has been comedy, so I do know how to time a laugh. It's a bit ironic, really.'

To John, a reaction he received at home was much more important. He went into the kitchen and found daughter Joanna watching *Home to Roost* on the video and laughing her head off. 'I think she was about twelve at the time and she said to me, "I often watch it when I get bored. If I want a laugh, I put it on." ' John was delighted; this was praise indeed.

One of the great missed opportunities of John Thaw's career was *Mitch*, the series that featured the actor as a hard-drinking London crime reporter. It should have been a powerful follow-up success to *The Sweeney*. Thaw was excellent in the role of the tough-talking reporter and the scripts from former *Sweeney* writer Roger Marshall sparkled with promise. But programme-makers London Weekend Television cut back the budget and then kept the shows on the shelf for almost two years, making them look dated and deeply irritating the star.

John put a great deal of effort into the production and said: 'I spent a lot of time with journalists before the series and I wouldn't mind being one if I had my time again.' Then he added darkly: 'Mitch is a very successful journalist and throughout the series his morality is questionable, but then a lot of guys are like that, aren't they?'

Although Mitch and Jack Regan operated in similar territory, on the fringes of London's lawless underworld, John Thaw and Roger Marshall went to great lengths to make them different. 'Regan would have thought Mitch was a pain in the neck,' Thaw said. 'I certainly didn't set out to recreate Regan. Mitch is written differently and he behaves differently.'

When it was finally screened, starting in August 1984, John Thaw was angry and disappointed. In a rare flash of public rage he stormed: 'We made it two years ago under the impression that it would be going out as we were making it. It has been held up for so long that I am afraid at least two of the episodes are now totally out of date. There came a time when I wondered if *Mitch* was ever going to be seen. I thought, "What did we all work our backsides off for?" It's not the money. I've been paid for it, after all. But we all worked very hard. They never gave me a reason. They never, as far I know, gave the producer a reason for not showing it. When we started I thought it was a good series and a good team making it. I thought that if people liked this first one we would go on and make two more series. Now there won't be any more. I think we were very badly treated.' London Weekend blamed scheduling difficulties, but in fact *Mitch* was a victim of both cash shortages and executive changes at LWT.

7

MORSE

Inspector Morse is melancholy about life, obsessive about his work, and frequently difficult with those closest to him. And after perhaps his most demanding day's filming his role as the world's most popular detective John Thaw admitted with a wry smile: 'Morse is the nearest character to myself I've ever played.'

John was relaxing with a glass of red wine in the remote Australian town of Cowra, an hour's flight inland from Sydney. That day he had spent the day in temperatures of up to 106 degrees in the shade. Only there was no shade out there, facing a demented gunman in the exceptional Morse adventure 'Promised Land', where the cerebral sleuth was on the trail of a relocated supergrass whose past was threatening to catch up with him violently.

Morse's beloved Oxford seemed a million miles away and there was not a *Times* crossword or a pint of real ale in sight. The scene was emotional and extraordinarily involved. Morse faced a desperately dangerous man who had seized a young girl prisoner down the length of a dusty railway track. The rehearsals and shooting took all day and John Thaw's presence and concentration never wavered once. The power behind the eyes was awesome to watch. After the complex scene was finally recorded, with the young hostage freed and the murderous gangster shot dead in a sequence that required Thaw to be splattered with TV blood, after hours exposed to the blazing sun, the star observed bluntly: 'If I don't get a hat on soon my brains will fry.'

Later, in a peaceful hotel garden, the actor explained his enduring affinity with the grumpy policeman. 'After playing Jack Regan in *The Sweeney* I thought I'd had it with cop shows. But *Morse* is different,' said John thoughtfully. 'When you consider how many cops there have been on television and in films it's amazing that Colin Dexter came up with such a fresh idea.

'As soon as I read it I knew it was so different from *The Sweeney* and so good that I was happy to do it. I could see it had a chance of being successful. I am very fond of the old bugger. Obviously looking at him as a person there is a lot wrong with him, but I am still very fond of him because I can understand why he is what he is, why he is the way he is, I should say. He is a sad guy in many ways, totally sad and he knows it inside. I am sure that when he shuts his door at night in his flat that there are a lot of nights, not every night perhaps, that he sits there and thinks, "Where am I?" His assistant Lewis has got a family and a home and a future, and he is a lot younger. It must make Morse compare their lives and ask himself where he is in life. He knows he is a sad man. But then when he wakes up next morning and thinks, "Oh, I must go and interview so and so, or talk to somebody else," and he starts working again he has his reason for living back. His work is his life. He gets busy and then becomes quite self-contained. That is his job with a capital J which makes him sad because his work is his whole life.'

John Thaw thought deeply about all the characters he

played but perhaps most about his portrayal of Morse. 'I am delighted he seems to have struck a chord with the viewers. Women particularly seem to take him to their hearts. Let's face it, there are a lot of women who don't like "police series" in inverted commas. But *Morse* is not like *Z Cars* or *The Sweeney*. They're stories. They're one-off films. Morse is first and foremost a man who happens to be a policeman, but he is also a rather sensitive, gentle man and I think that is why women quite like him. Maybe they want to look after him. He is very lonely in his flat, even with his music. I think I know what that sort of life is like. I have had periods in my life when I have been a bachelor. After my first marriage broke up I had a period of about eighteen months when I lived on my own. I am not quite such a loner as Morse, but I do know what it is like to come home to an empty flat. He is not me. He is a copper and he has a brilliant brain, which I certainly do not have. But in lots of ways I can understand why he is what he is. He is much more complicated than the usual television copper, and we don't get bogged down in all that tedious police procedure. I was interested in Morse because he's not a cliché copper any more than Regan was. The guy's brain is working all the time. He has a mind like an intellectual grasshopper which made him challenging to play. But if Morse had been like Regan, chasing and fighting villains, I would not have done it because it would have been too close to going over old ground. Morse doesn't like violence and goes out of his way to avoid it. I also liked the fact that Morse is not always right, so that even when he thinks he has cracked it, the viewers can't be sure. But I am not a "lovey-darling" sort of actor. To me it's a job. I do it for money in exactly the same way that a carpenter makes things with wood for money. Although I am very fond of

Morse, the old bugger. I never liked traditional heroes. I never wanted to play Hamlet or Romeo, I always wanted to be Iago.'

John happily admits to sharing some of Morse's characteristics. They both love classical music and they both hate hospitals. And they are both very squeamish. As the actor said: 'There was a scene in the morgue where the body of a girl had to be pulled out of the freezer. The smell of the morgue and the way the actress was made up to look like a dead body was very eerie. I just wanted to get the hell out of there. He is flawed in certain areas and he makes mistakes all the time. He is human and vulnerable. But I wouldn't want to cross him. He is very clever and quick and of course he can be snobbish and patronizing. There is much more of me in Morse than ever there was in Regan. I'm quieter and I love classical music. And I certainly don't kick doors down. Morse is the nearest thing to me I've ever played.'

Morse and Thaw are both men of much mood and few words. Thaw talks about Morse as one would a faintly tiresome relative you can't ignore. As if he met him he would find him intimidating. 'He's sensitive, but he's also pompous and arrogant, qualities I don't go for.' Yet the similarities between the two men are there for all to see. They both have an uncompromising integrity, a shyness that is sometimes used as a defence mechanism, and a lack of patience with the fallibilities of others that makes neither man want to suffer fools gladly.

The attention the character brought was less welcome. Thaw observed: 'There I am in the supermarket trying to choose between spaghetti and tagliatelli and someone is saying, "You know the one when the body was in the cupboard, it wasn't really him, was it?" I nod and smile and walk away.'

The Australian adventure showed John Thaw's determination never to rest on his laurels and always attempt to raise his sights and his standards. He said: 'I had been trying for years to get Morse out of Oxford. The original producer Kenny McBain and I had plans to go to Canada, to Holland and even to Russia at one time.'

John was so single-minded when he was working that it was possible to get under his skin. A young photographer covering the shoot waited for his moment and a break in filming, but when it arrived he made the mistake of asking the star if he would, 'Act a bit.' The response was a chunky script which hit the photographer on the side of the head. John Thaw did not suffer fools gladly.

The local police covering the tiny country town of Cowra certainly took a great interest in the influx of television folk. 'The motel owners were pleased to see us but I'm not so sure about the police,' said producer David Lascelles. 'An awful lot of us seemed to get pulled up and breathalysed so we had to be on our best behaviour in the evening.'

Thaw did not suffer from the drink-drive spotlight. He drank only sparingly then, and in any case spent most evenings in his motel room learning his mammoth allocation of lines. Britain's most popular policeman was still thoughtful enough to attempt to keep Stafford Hildred, one of the writers, out of the clutches of the law. After we had shared the wine he politely declined a lift back to his hotel. 'I'll get a cab,' he said. 'And you be careful if you're driving. Don't go over the bridge on the main road, that's an obvious place for them to be waiting. I'd hate for you to come all this way to interview a TV policeman and then finish up getting nicked by a real one.'

The *High Noon*-style shootout that provided the climax

surprised even Thaw. When he read the script he told the writer, Julian Mitchell, that he had: 'More front than Selfridges!' After four years of high-quality, top-rating drama the programme-makers were perfectly happy to keep producing more of the same, but John Thaw believed in surprising his audience from time to time. He enthused: 'I love Australia. I love the people and I love the country. I wanted to bring Morse out here to bring a new dimension to the series. I wanted to take him out of his closed environment of Oxford and put him in a vast country where he doesn't have his familiar surroundings like his books and his car, and see how he would cope. I thought it would provide a new look at an established character that would be interesting.

'For me it worked because the great outdoors of the Australian countryside was a world away from the academic background of Oxford. Morse was slightly flummoxed by the heat and by the Australian people, who are so straight and open. Australians tend to say what they mean straight off, while Morse tends to say ten words when one will suffice. It was an interesting situation and a cracking story and like all good ideas it is based on truth: an officer like Morse could well be sent to question a grass on the other side of the world if necessary.'

In this case Morse and Lewis were on the trail of one Kenny Stone, whose evidence helped to put away a gang of armed robbers who had killed a policeman friend of Morse several years earlier. One of the gang had died in prison of AIDS and the death sparked a media campaign to reopen the case. It also highlighted the differences between Morse and Lewis. While Morse was uncomfortable in the heat, Lewis was in his element with the unstuffy Australians and the wide-open spaces.

Like Morse, John Thaw missed his home very badly. The

actor shyly confessed: 'I don't like being away from home but sometimes it is part of the job. Sheila always says, "Enjoy it, enjoy it," which I know is good advice, especially when you're in such a beautiful part of the world as this, but I find it hard. Some people thrive on being away and steam into whatever is happening, but I am not one of them. I virtually count the days until I get home again. I'm afraid I don't even use the time to write long letters home. I wrote a letter to Sheila last week and it was such an unusual thing for me to do she said she was going to have it framed! It'll be worth a fortune when I'm dead. That's how often I write.'

The trip also gave John the chance to visit his brother Raymond, who lives with his family in Brisbane and works as a foreman for Ford's. The brothers have always remained very close despite the miles that separate them and the visit was a happy one. John said afterwards that he deeply regretted the fact they lived on opposite sides of the world but he could understand his brother's love of the Aussie lifestyle. 'Ray emigrated with his wife more than thirty years ago on the ten-pound assisted passage. His children were born there. So although he is very much an Anglophile, staying up all night to watch English football, I don't suppose they will return to England.'

The startling *Inspector Morse* TV success story began some four years before Morse went Down Under. Morse first drove on to our screens in his beloved maroon Jaguar 2.4 on 6 January 1987. In a film called 'The Dead of Jericho' he was taking his classic car to the garage on his way to a choir rehearsal when he ran into some villains in a hurry and the Jag was cruelly crumpled. Straight away Morse steered his audience into a complex and compelling drama involving suspicious suicide, adultery, blackmail, a peeping Tom and a gay drug addict who blinded himself. The pattern of quality crime films was established from the outset.

The viewers loved it from the start. Audiences began at just under 15 million and have remained very high throughout. The series broke ITV ratings records for drama. Even knowing whodunnit does not deter loyal *Morse* fans, as the repeats of the series are often watched by audiences of more than 12 million. *Morse* always attracts massive figures and in 1990 it was the most watched drama on both ITV and on Channel 4.

Morse is popular in Australia, America and also in such diverse countries as Bulgaria, Mongolia and Zambia. Even workers on Britain's North Sea oil rigs demand to have *Morse* helicoptered out on video and the United States Department of Defense has bought the series to show on closed-circuit television to servicemen. John Thaw's powerful portrayal of the melancholy bachelor policeman has switched on a worldwide audience approaching 1 billion people.

Thaw's partnership with Kevin Whately as his steadfast but endlessly harassed sidekick Sergeant Lewis was a television success story that lasted fifteen years. But John always remembered the debt he owed to writer Colin Dexter. 'It all starts with a story,' he said simply. 'Without a good story I might as well not bother to turn up for work.' Thaw understood that people enjoy police series because they enjoy a good mystery. 'You can hang a good story on a detective or a policeman. It's not the police *per se* that people like, but you couldn't make a very exciting series about a gardener.' Thaw knew that compared to the real lives of serving police officers *Morse* is in 'Fairyland', but smiled to himself when a senior policeman said to him, 'Keep on doing Morse, it's so good for our image.'

Morse's name was inspired by Sir Jeremy Morse, chairman of Lloyd's Bank and a crossword champion much admired by crossword compiler Dexter. 'I didn't base Morse on Sir Jeremy,' said the writer. 'But when I was searching for names for the characters in my first Morse book I chose people I admired. C J Morse, as he was then, and Mrs B Lewis, the pseudonym used by Dorothy Taylor, who sets the *Observer* newspaper crossword, were the two people I admired most in the crossword world.'

Morse's love of Wagner, crosswords, beer and women are all shared by the author. The dry, down-to-earth Dexter wit is in there as well. 'Morse can be mean,' admits Dexter. 'I think one of the great crimes is to be reluctant to buy your round.'

The murder mysteries featuring Inspector Morse have generated book sales measured in their millions in seventeen languages around the world. Yet the man behind the melancholy, middle-aged detective can't for the life of him understand what all the fuss is about. With worldwide earnings hurtling into the stratosphere, Colin Dexter simply refuses to get excited. He possesses a world-weary equanimity which helped to turn his working partnership with John Thaw into a lasting friendship. Neither man allows his work to dominate his life. 'There are far more important things in life than a few detective stories,' said the mild-mannered Oxford academic who passed on many of his own thoughtful personality traits to his TV hero. Dexter still lives in the same unremarkable semi that he bought when his main source of income was setting Oxford University examinations, drives a humble H-registration Citroën and declines to holiday abroad.

'The money makes no difference at all to me,' says the former schoolmaster who turned to exam setting when his deafness forced him from the classroom. 'I was happy enough on a teacher's salary.' The house is homely and comfortable yet starkly furnished, and the bookshelves are stacked with the works of Plato, Socrates and Homer. However, unlike the charismatic Morse, Colin Dexter is certainly no lonely bachelor. He and his wife Dorothy have been married for more than forty years.

Dexter's cerebral sleuth first sprang into life on paper on a family holiday to Wales in 1972. He recalled: 'It was raining and I had just read a novel I thought was lousy so I sat down to write a better one. That was the beginning of *Last Bus to Woodstock*, a story about a detective called Morse. If you start writing fiction you're going to start writing about yourself, as that is someone you know fairly well. So I made Morse interested in things I'm interested in, like beer and Wagner and crosswords and women.

'I certainly did not know anything about the details of police procedure. When I started writing Morse I had only ever been inside a police station twice in my life. Both times to report a stolen bicycle.

'But above all I wanted to make him a very clever man – which is easy enough in a book, but a very hard thing to show on television. It was all very gradual. I never looked on writing as a way to make money, I had a good job already. I was so glad when Macmillan agreed to publish the first one – I would have paid them, I think. After that first success the publishers wanted more. I used to write in between listening to *The Archers* and going out to the pub.

'You see, if you write just page a day you write three hundred and sixty-five pages a year. I used to nip out for a drink with a dear old friend called John Poole on whom I based the character of the pathologist Max in the earlier books. He was a very distinguished doctor himself and was quite amused by that.'

John Thaw brilliantly conveyed Morse's solitary pessimism, a trait that TV viewers find so endlessly appealing. Colin Dexter was delighted with his star: 'We have done thirty-one films so far and some of them have been better than others, but John has always given a hundred per cent. I think he shares some of my gloomy views on the state of the universe and he can appear very vulnerable and melancholy, which is just right for the character.

'I think all three of us – Morse and me and John – are somewhat pessimistic about the future of the world, and I think this slight sadness comes through. John does that wonderfully well. I am genuinely a little gloomy about the future. There's not much hope for us at all.' He smiled. 'I don't see how anyone can be optimistic these days.

'John Thaw is a very professional man. I was thrilled when he accepted the role. He is always anxious to do his job to the best of his ability. He always puts that first. I think he enjoys the character of Morse. He plays him with such conviction and aplomb. If he had no sympathy with the character then the series would never have achieved the success it has. He is always conscious of the work the other actors, the writer and the production team put in, and always quick to sing their praises.'

Dexter had nothing to do with choosing John Thaw to play his hero but his mental picture of Morse was very close to the actor. 'When I created Morse I wanted someone who was extraordinarily clever, cerebrally alpha plus. Anyone who gets to know John finds he is a relaxed, gentle person. But he is extraordinarily intelligent and interesting to talk to and not nearly so rude as Morse. Of course John is not the morose character that Morse is, but he does have a slight melancholy cast to his face. There is a sympathy towards Morse. John is nothing like as gloomy as Morse but there is an undercurrent of melancholia in John's own life.'

When the actor first took on the role he went to meet the writer and asked him dozens of questions about the inspector's lifestyle. Where did he live? Why there? How long had he been there? What sort of furniture did he have? Dexter was flattered to be asked to help an actor build up the character he was playing. 'For an actor any background helps,' explained Thaw. 'It all adds colour. I'm delighted with the way Colin's high-quality writing has lifted the series.'

'But then,' continued Dexter, 'Morse has all sorts of stupid qualities. He's mean with money. Lewis always has to fork out for the drinks, for instance. He is often very cross and impatient and unfair with his subordinates. In fact he really has a lot of objectionable qualities – unlike John. But I think Morse is popular because people don't know exactly what makes him tick. And they are fascinated by the way he approaches things. John is above all a very private person. He is very easy with people he knows but he doesn't suffer fools gladly. He can be quiet and shy, but once you've got to know him you realize what a great sense of humour he has.

'On one occasion in Oxford's Randolph Hotel, Morse had to down a pint of beer,' said Dexter. 'John doesn't even like drinking beer but he braved it anyway. Then they discovered that something was wrong in the shot and he had to do it a second time. Then someone noticed that the clock was showing the wrong time, so poor John had to drink a third pint. When he did it he got a round of applause from the film crew. But then, no matter how difficult the job, John is always cool and professional. He never brings his personal problems on set with him. Even when his wife was very ill with cancer he never gave in. John did not have the advantages I had when I was a child. He is not a university man like Morse. It was his overwhelming talent that got him to RADA.'

Colin Dexter grew up in Stamford in Lincolnshire where his father was a taxi driver and his mother worked in a butcher's shop. 'They both left school at twelve,' he said, 'but they encouraged me and my brother to work hard and we both did well at school and went to Cambridge University.' After Cambridge, Dexter served in the army as a signalman for his National Service. 'I went to Germany where I was very good at high speed Morse,' he said with a twinkle of a grin.

'After the army I taught Latin and Greek until my hearing deteriorated. I went deaf and in 1966 I came to Oxford. Dorothy and I both fell in love with the city and we have been happy here ever since.' The beautiful city makes a marvellous backdrop for Morse, and Dexter's proudest possession is a commendation from the Lord Mayor for writing so elegantly about Town and Gown, rather than just the famous university.

Colin Dexter is seventy-two now: 'Long past bus pass time,' he says. And he is not planning to go on for ever. But he still enjoys his Alfred Hitchcock-style walk-on appearances in almost every Morse adventure. They were instigated by the first producer, Kenny McBain, as a tribute which has become a Morse in-joke. John Thaw recalls: 'Kenny just said to Colin, "Why don't you walk down that corridor." He was petrified and I saw him and did a double take.' Dexter prefers to make his fleeting personal appearance as a pub customer, because of his enduring enthusiasm for real ale.

'It has been a long haul, you can't keep on doing it for ever. I find it harder and harder to get the inclination to write. I don't think you get older and better for ever as a writer. I have never wanted to buy a yacht or go and live in California or the south of France. I don't like going abroad much. The money is not important – I've always had enough money.

'Even though Morse and I will always be fairly miserable, if I'm honest I have to say it's been a lot of fun. Morse Tours and Morse Walks are a bit over the top, but I suppose it's quite an accolade. Pubs are always asking me for bits of manuscript, and they have Morse beer in the Randolph.'

The crucial conversation in bringing Inspector Morse to our screens was between Ted Childs, then the highly respected Controller of Drama at Central Television, and young producer Kenny McBain, who was in charge of Michael Elphick's popular *Boon* series. Childs, whose long association with Thaw had already given viewers *The Sweeney*, was on the lookout for a more thoughtful crime series. He much admired the stylish quality of the BBC's *Miss Marple* and mentioned his feelings to McBain, who replied: 'I've been reading these novels by Colin Dexter. They feature a detective and they're set in Oxford.'

The rest was not quite history because the inspirational producer believed passionately that, to do them justice, the Inspector Morse stories had to be told over two hours, then a revolutionary concept for ITV bosses always impatient for the quick fix of instant ratings which had traditionally come from hour-long adventures. Childs agreed that the subtle and demanding stories required more screen time but then had to battle hard to win the day. The accepted television wisdom at the time was that ITV viewers would not be gripped by complicated stories lasting as long as a feature film. But Childs's impressive track record and his passionate eloquence were convincing. He put the idea to John Thaw, and after asking a lot of questions and for time to think it over the star was convinced. Thaw said simply: 'Ted believes in quality television and so do I. So I listened.'

The wise and vastly experienced executive knew the actor was crucial to the project. Childs explained: 'John Thaw is the sort of person people would like to have as a father or a lover. He has this great sympathy. Look at Morse. If you read that character on the page you would think, "What a miserable sod!" In the wrong hands it could have been a tedious portrayal. But John is able to make the character appealing. In his hands Morse is a flawed hero who evinces sympathy rather than uninterest. You want him to win. Morse is like Sam Spade, an alien figure who is capable of establishing a rapport with the audience.'

The respect between Thaw and Childs was definitely mutual. Thaw said: 'Ted is a good bloke and he knows what he is talking about when it comes to television. Ted was the one who bought *Morse* before there was a script. The best thing about old Ted, whom I've known for many years, is that he never pressures you. It was a big gamble running each story for two hours. Ted has a memo from someone saying this was the worst idea ever and that no viewer would stick with it. This memo writer has since left the company,' added John with a wry smile.

There was insufficient film capacity in Central's Birmingham studios at the time so the company's film-making arm, Zenith, was handed the job with Childs, who described Morse as 'a thinking man's Columbo', retaining control and McBain as producer. At the time the Zenith bosses were reluctant to take on a series of two-hour detective stories, although once the project was a success they were delighted to trumpet the triumph. However, John always knew whom he was working for. 'It makes me laugh sometimes now when I feel that Zenith are trying to take the credit,' said the actor. 'It was Ted and Kenny and Central who believed in the show when Zenith weren't at all keen on the idea of making our two-hour films. I don't forget that.'

Thaw was doing a Ray Cooney farce, *Two Into One*, in Toronto and not really enjoying the experience when he was offered the part of Morse. The fact Morse was so different to Regan was an attraction, but there were aspects of Morse that John Thaw definitely did not like, which were quickly and quietly dropped from the television character.

Morse's inclination to react to attractive female witnesses works perfectly well in Dexter's novels, but Thaw felt unhappy about portraying it on screen. The sexual side of the lonely bachelor was discreetly played down. The clever crimefighter started life as a sex-obsessed loner, who sometimes allowed his lusts to get in the way of his detective work. But Thaw refused to play the seamier side of Morse from Dexter's original novels and insisted on cleaning up his private life. He said emphatically: 'I didn't like the seedy side of Morse in the early books. He was a bit of a dirty old man. I didn't like that and I wouldn't play it. I hated the fact that he was sometimes rude to women and I told the writers I wanted that changed. I wanted him to be more sensitive.'

In Dexter's first Morse story, *Last Bus to Woodstock*, the

libidinous side of Morse's character is given a very free rein. In print Morse fantasizes about women covered in blood, worries about falling in love too often and has a passionate fling with a beautiful murderess. But when the adventure was televised, John's Morse kept his distance from the females involved and no explicit scenes were included. He explained: 'When I was Jack Regan in *The Sweeney* I had all the women, but I wanted Morse to be completely different. *Morse* is much more demanding for an actor than *The Sweeney*, because you've got to keep the interest going when there is very little happening visually. At his best he does seem to touch something in people. One American woman wrote to say that she thinks he's sad because of all the evil he has seen, and he does seem to have that aura about him.'

Morse is definitely very popular with female viewers but any references to his remarkable sex appeal were guaranteed to make the actor wince with embarrassment: 'Whenever there is something in the press about me being the sexiest man on television or some such rubbish, Sheila and the girls all laugh. Quite rightly. What they mean is that Morse is sexy, not me. I used to get lots of letters from women on *The Sweeney*, as I do on *Morse*, and although they all start "Dear John" those women are really writing to Regan or Morse.'

However, Thaw appreciated why women find Morse so attractive: 'It's nothing to do with the way he looks – just the way he is. He likes women, he's sensitive and romantic and he doesn't hide it if he is attracted to someone, but he's also a challenge. Women see him as the eternal bachelor, they think they can change him but he's so set in his ways it's impossible. With Morse women either go along with his lifestyle or get out.'

Sharon Maughan played a radio phone-in agony aunt in the Morse story 'Deceived by Flight' and she was left in no doubt as to the appeal of the man. 'You don't have to be a beefcake to be sexy,' said Sharon. 'I see John as an English Spencer Tracy – white-haired, sensitive and extremely charming. He's someone with character and inner strength. Quite obviously he has the ability to make women go all weak at the knees. What John has created is very sexy. He has made Inspector Morse his own. Morse might be Colin Dexter's creation, but it's John who has breathed life into him.

'Morse brings out the maternal instinct in women. There's a sort of overwhelming urge to trap him. He drinks too much, he makes mistakes, and he is the sort who needs looking after. He's also very charismatic and clever. Oh yes, I quite understand his sex appeal.' Morse's failure to find a soul-mate just adds to his allure, says Sharon. 'Loneliness is a self-perpetuating habit. I don't think Morse really wants to be successful in love.'

Another major change from the books was the car. Dexter originally had Morse driving round in a Lancia but John Thaw and the producers agreed it would be better to go British on screen and they plumped for the aged Jaguar. John said: 'That car is almost a character in itself, particularly when it goes wrong. We have spent thousands of pounds on the engine and the bodywork but getting it started could sometimes be a real problem. That caused an awful lot of retakes. We had a mechanic full time who always seemed to have his bum sticking out from under the bonnet. It's a pig to drive, though. It's like driving a bus before they brought in power steering.'

From the beginning John Thaw was very protective of the screen character. He refused ever to allow him to swear or blaspheme. In the Australian story he even removed the word 'Christ' from his lines. 'Morse would not say that,' he insisted firmly. And Thaw insists old-fashioned gentleman Morse would always be very courteous to women. He said: 'In one episode a writer had Morse grabbing a woman. There is no way he would do that sort of thing, so I didn't do it.

'I don't think any of us expected it to be the success it has been. The main thing I hear from people is that the programme length of two hours gives them the chance to get involved with the characters and the relationships which develop between them.

'The fact that Morse is not a slick character and has his own problems is a lot to do with his appeal. He is the thinking man's detective. People seem to like his thoughtful, non-violent approach. I think viewers are fed-up with car chases and shoot-outs. They like Morse because he is a more cerebral character who sees each case as a battle of wits.'

John was delighted that Morse received such a warm reception from the public and the critics but characteristically refused to get too excited. He said: 'I never get big-headed about acting. It's a job – what else can it be? I don't live my life through Morse. I've been in this game for more than thirty years and if I can't tell the difference now between what is my job and what is my real life, I never will. I've had praise before and I've had prizes before and there is no way I believe all the hype.'

The only part of Morse that the actor really envied is his intellect. 'To be truthful, I do feel intimidated by academic people, even at my ripe old age. I feel stupid, or should I say inferior, when I'm talking to knowledgeable people. I feel that if I knew half of what they know I'd be a different person. I could have done so many other things and led a much richer life.

'But I know for a fact that the reverse applies. Some academics look at me and wish they had been an actor, appeared in a series like *Morse* and won awards. I have to say that I think I would be terrified if I ever met Inspector Morse. I wouldn't want to cross him. He lives on a pretty short fuse and he's very clever, very well read and he lets everyone know, given half a chance.

'Sheila always says that if she had her life again she would have gone to university. The difference between us is that she was bright enough to do that, but I was not clever enough, or perhaps too lazy, to take advantage of what education I had. When I talk about university, I'm talking fairytales. It's the equivalent of my saying I wish I could run the four-minute mile – it just wasn't within my reach.'

If John Thaw's intellect had its limitations, his strength of character was always of the very highest quality. The leading man of *Inspector Morse* has always led his team from the front. Actress Anna Calder Marshall was working on an episode of *Morse* alongside John at the time Sheila Hancock's breast cancer was discovered. She said afterwards: 'It happened at the same time that Kenny McBain died of cancer. John was incredibly strong. Everyone on the programme was terribly concerned about Kenny but John gave everyone strength.'

Anna played an Oxford don whom Morse was keen on, though typically his affection was not returned. She said: 'Morse is different things to different women. He's the strong silent type, but there is also a rough quality to him. He is very much a man and you feel protected when you are with him, both by the actor and the character he plays.

I think there is a bit of Morse in John. He is undoubtedly very attractive to women and at the same time he seems a bit of a loner.'

Jan Harvey, who appeared in 'Greeks Bearing Gifts', believes vulnerability is the key to the Morse magic. 'You have a sense that his past is one of pain and isolation,' she said. 'It's the sort of character that makes you want to build bridges towards it. And then there is the element of surprise – an unexpected culture, a sudden gentleness. But of course John Thaw is much too good an actor to let you know which, if any, of these qualities are his.'

Not all of John's co-stars were prepared to admire him from a distance. One beautiful actress, who was thirty-seven when she appeared in *Inspector Morse*, was totally smitten. She said: 'I completely fell for him and made a bit of a fool of myself. I had been going through a very difficult time at home and on the morning of the read-through my long-term partner had just crashed out of the house for good.

'Echoes of our last, bitter row were still going round in my head as I sat in this room with all these strangers, trying to make sense of a script that seemed desperately obscure to me. I tried to concentrate but to be honest I couldn't make much sense of it all. I wasn't sure whether my character was good or bad and I'm sure my problems showed in my voice.

'When we broke for coffee I just sat and stared straight ahead and tried to get myself together. Then John brought a mug of coffee over and smiled at me. I can still remember that smile. He has such a wonderful, lived-in face that so often looks a bit sad that when he smiles it's like a ray of light. He just said, "Old Morse can be a shade complex when you first try to get to grips with him." And I melted.

He was so understanding and so kind. I thought I had just about managed to keep my inner turmoil to myself, but, although we had never met, John knew that something was wrong with me.

'I started to blurt out some apologies about my leaden performance and he just said, "Don't worry, you'll be fine. This is only the read-through. It's best to save it for the camera." Then he changed the subject and he started to tell me who people were, taking the mickey in that lovely, easy way. I realized he was trying to draw me into the group, who all seemed to know each other like old friends. It was so kind. Afterwards I couldn't get him out of my mind.

'The next time we met was on location in north London. As soon as he saw me he came across and called me by my character's name and made a joke about what an old woman the director was being that day. He included me and he didn't have to do that. He had pages of dialogue to worry about in some very demanding scenes.

'After that I made rather a fool of myself. Those twinkling blue eyes seemed to be saying that we might be more than friends and I felt as though I was about sixteen as I considered the prospect. John Thaw is not drop-dead handsome like some actors I've worked with but he just has this enormous sex appeal. I was still very lonely and unhappy at home and I started to fantasize about us getting together. I would make a beeline for him whenever there was a break in filming.

'I thought he would be prickly and awkward to talk to but he was the exact opposite. He was light and funny and seemed interested in my life. We had an old friend in common and he gently teased me about an old relationship. I remember blushing like a schoolgirl and thinking I really wanted him. The next morning I took an age getting

ready to go to work and promised myself I would somehow get a little closer.

'But I blew it. I laughed just a little too loud. And then
when we were talking together after lunch I just touched
his arm. That did it. He suddenly tensed up as though
someone had blasted a thousand volts through his body
and I saw a mist go over his eyes. I knew in that moment
that I had tried too hard. I had got too close. I can still
remember that awful feeling of disappointment as I realized he did not feel the same way as me. Nothing was said
but I never shared another minute with him. He was
always somewhere else and I was added to the no doubt
long list of predatory females.

'Still, that's nearer than most women get. And in my
hopeless, unrequited love for John Thaw I had forgotten
about the shiftless former lover, who was by then leaving
whining messages of regret on my answerphone. The best
thing is I have nothing to feel guilty for. Millions of women
television viewers dream of sensitive, attractive men like
John Thaw. I don't blame them. He'll always have a special
place in my heart. The memory of those eyes still makes
me go tingly.'

Morse's partnership with the long-suffering Detective
Sergeant Lewis, played by Kevin Whately, has always been
central to the appeal of the programme. Lewis is changed
even more from the original than Morse. In Dexter's books
he is much older than on screen, with grown-up children
and a Welsh wife. But on screen Whately became the perfect
foil as a younger man, forever anxious to get home to his
young wife and family. The actor wisely saw the contrasts
between Morse and Lewis and used his considerable talents
to make the double act fresh and interesting. He spurned
the fashionable buddy-buddy relationship, remembering

the important facts that Morse was older, higher-ranking and intellectually on a different plane.

After his long success with Dennis Waterman in *The Sweeney*, John Thaw was delighted to find a second partner he respected and enjoyed working with. A dozen actors were auditioned for the plum role but Whately's youthful honest appeal was what won him the part, along with his acting talent. John said: 'We wanted an earnest, almost innocent, younger chap to contrast with old Morse. I met Kevin for the first time at the start. We did not know each other before *Inspector Morse* and we hit it off right from the beginning. In the books Lewis is a much older man, a grandfather, but Kenny McBain had the idea of making him a much younger man than Morse and I think it works very well that way. We have a lot of scenes together and we find that we can convey emotions with a glance. It worked well right from the start because Kevin is a very responsive actor. He works out very quickly what is needed and joins in. He is very intuitive, like me. Although Morse is grumpy and demanding with Lewis I think he is very fond of him. He would be lost without him.' Even so, you feel the two men always keep their distance. In all the saga surrounding the mystery of Morse's secret first name it may have escaped many viewers' notice that Lewis's first name is Rob and that it took five years of working together before Morse ever used it.

Kevin Whately will always be grateful for the reduction in Lewis's age as *Inspector Morse* transferred from page to screen. 'That decision worked out nicely for me,' said the cheery Geordie actor. 'It's a pleasure and an education to work with John Thaw. Even though we had not met before, we seemed to have a kind of chemistry from the start. John is great to work with. At first he used to help and advise me a lot because I had hardly worked on film. He has amazing concentration. He just sort of burns under the camera. I love the way the screen relationship has developed a little more each series. At time goes on, Lewis is less and less subservient and becomes just a bit bolshie. I reckon this is probably what would happen in real life. Lewis surely wouldn't stand for being put down for ever. But it is such a successful formula we don't really want to change a thing.'

When they flew to Australia to film 'Promised Land' the two actors arrived in Sydney a few days early. 'John and I met up some time before work started and just tootled around the harbour in boats and sat drinking beer on Manly Beach. John's not really a beer drinker, in spite of Morse's enthusiasm for real ale, but he was choking down the Aussie stuff all right!'

Morse's screen view on Australian beer was typically forthright. In the film he took one sip, pulled a face, and said: 'They don't spell it with four Xs for nothing.'

Kevin Whately has no illusions about the secret of the popularity of *Inspector Morse*. He said: 'I think the whole success of *Morse* is down to John. I know there's a high standard of writing, the music is good, and Oxford looks lovely, but the main thing is, even at our steady pace, John is always watchable.'

It was John's talent as a mimic which helped to keep Kevin chuckling while they worked. The caravan they shared on location has been known to rock with laughter from within on more than one occasion. 'People think John's so serious but often he's just the opposite,' said Kevin. 'He has a very zany sense of humour. If anybody has a quirk John is so fast at picking it up. He is superb at dialects. He is very impish and hardly anyone escapes his impersonations.

John Thaw

And he is accurate, too. But always good-humoured. I could never stand up on stage and tell jokes. John could. I don't suppose he would want to, but he could be a stand-up comic, I am sure. He does concentrate tremendously hard on the part but he loves a laugh as well. He can mimic just about every voice and he is a great story-teller, while I am a good listener. Maybe that helps us to be a team.

'I'm a very shy bloke. I think I only went into acting in the first place because it helped me to cope with my shyness. I'm fine if I've got a character to hide behind.'

John Thaw and Kevin Whately have both made many friends among the ranks of genuine policemen who figure prominently among the fans of *Inspector Morse*. 'We've got particularly friendly with the police in Oxford, where the series is set. They like it a lot because it doesn't sensational-ize what they do. Morse and Lewis are not stereotypes. And I believe our two-hour format gives us and the writers the chance to explore the personalities properly. The viewing figures are good in Britain and it is sold all over the world so we must be doing something right.'

Millions of the new fans were in the United States, where *Morse* attracted a following who saw the gentle whodunnit series as the perfect antidote to the violence in many American drama series. John Thaw was delighted with the response from across the Atlantic: 'We've been getting a lot of fanmail from the States. When we're film-ing in Oxford a lot of American tourists come up and tell us how much they enjoy *Morse*. And when I went to America the television critics told me that viewers there particularly liked *Morse* because it was not all car chases and violence. They liked the tranquillity and the very English manner of *Morse*.'

In real life the two actors became close friends but they

tended not to socialize outside their long working hours. 'When we finish he goes home and I go home,' said John. 'He's pretty stubborn, old Kevin, you know. I don't know much more about Kevin now than I did when we first started and what I do know is what I have asked him direct. Kevin plays his cards pretty close to his chest. But during our working day we are good mates. I know it can appear a bit of a one-man show because Morse does have the lion's share of the dialogue and seems to be in just about every scene, but I think of it as much more of a part-nership. Lewis is a very vital part of *Morse*, a key ingredient of the success of the show.

'I was very lucky in *The Sweeney* with Dennis Waterman. Kevin is not like Dennis at all as a man, but again I think I am very lucky to get such a good partner. One of the reasons I have got on so well with both of them is that we all share a similar sense of humour. You need that if you're going to work well together and Kevin has a very good sense of humour.'

John was delighted when Kevin became assertive enough to insist on developing Lewis's character. The older actor said: 'If you compare the early *Morse*s with the later ones you can see that Lewis is now much more involved. I think Kevin got fed-up, quite rightly, of Lewis being a bit of a lemon. I think he had a bit of a word and said, "Let him fight back and stop being such a doormat for this arrogant man." They became much more of a part-nership than they were.'

8

BEYOND MORSE

The huge success of *Morse* did, however, take its toll on John Thaw. The schedule was punishing and by the end of series four he was feeling the strain. He said: 'In 1990, between *Morse* series four and *Morse* series five, I quite deliberately took some time off work. And I was so bored I just wanted to run to work. I was like an athlete who had been told he could not run for a month, or five months in my case. I had from January to May off work. We had a holiday in Siena but I did nothing a lot of the time. I decided to take the time off because I felt I had been pushing it too hard. It's difficult in our business to regulate how hard you'll work, but I said no to quite a few things, because I thought it would be good to wake up in the morning for a while and not feel I had any professional responsibilities.

'That was fine for about four weeks and then I began to feel, "I want to go somewhere and work". I began to see for the first time how people must feel when they are made redundant or forced to retire. It must be awful when you're used to going to an office or a factory or whatever. You get real withdrawal symptoms about not being at work, you

154

miss having something to do and people to talk to. Unfortunately Sheila was quite busy. We all went out to Siena and she was only there for two days before she had to fly off to Los Angeles to do some filming on *Three Men and a Little Lady*. I was with my daughters so we still went round and had a good time. But she was only in America for three days and when she came back we went to Florence.

'The trouble is it seems virtually impossible to get our holidays to coincide if we are both working. If we want to have a holiday together it means at least one of us has to say, "I will make sure I don't work." '

In the fifth series we even got to see Lewis's frequently mentioned family. Kevin Whateley noted: 'Sergeant Lewis's wife had appeared before, but only in shadow. She was played by a walk-on actress but this time she appears in three films and actually has some lines. The actress is Maureen Bennett, who went to the same drama school as me years ago.'

For all John Thaw's generous appreciation of Kevin Whately's contribution there was never any doubt in anyone's mind as to who was the real boss of the production. By the time the Australian film was being made Kevin had confided to John that he felt he had had enough of the role. But John Thaw has not reached his position in the business without developing a steely will of his own. He said firmly: 'Kevin is a wonderful actor and we make a very good contrasting pair, a good duo. And we get on very well, he's a good mate. I know that he is beginning to wonder if we haven't gone full cycle with the roles. But I don't know if I agree. Let's put it this way, I am not going to go into the next series thinking or saying it will be the last, because we get good scripts, we get wonderful back-up from the crew. There are not many places in television where you get the sort of support that *Morse* enjoys. So if you're doing good-quality work that people like and turn on to watch then I'm not about to sit in an Australian garden and say, "That's it. I've had enough of that." It's too precious these days to throw away. Kevin has told me that next year will be his last. If that happens, it's sad but "Bye Bye Kevin." We'll go on if I want to go on.'

Morse's splendid isolation in his flat with his crosswords and his music has always been an important part of the appeal of the character. And while John Thaw always insisted females were kept at arm's length, that did not prevent the detective from being attracted. Thaw admitted: 'Morse did become fond of the pathologist Dr Grayling Russell, played by Amanda Hillwood. But it couldn't possibly have worked. You couldn't have Morse married. You can't have him working on a case and then rushing off to the path. lab to see her for ten minutes. Getting married just wouldn't be Morse and you couldn't have him living with a woman. So, script-wise, they decided there was no future for the relationship so she had to go.'

By 1992, however, the programme-makers decided viewers needed to know a little more about the reasons behind Morse's solitary state. In his impressionable youth it seems Morse had been badly hurt by a woman at university. In 'Dead on Time' Joanna David, who is married to actor Edward Fox, played Susan Fallon, an old flame who devastated Morse by walking out on him. The shock meeting shattered both parties. John noted: 'I know viewers are intrigued by the lone nature of Morse and the film begins to help to explain why he is like he is. He finds he still carries a torch for Susan and he actually manages to tell her. Joanna was very good in the role, but it doesn't work out, of course. Being Morse, it never can, really. He always reaches out but the ball moves away when he is about to grab it.'

In spite of the unhappy ending Joanna David thoroughly enjoyed the experience. 'I felt very honoured,' she said. 'It must be every actress's dream to play the woman in Inspector Morse's life. I know there are millions of Morse-holics. I'm one and I'm sure fans want to find out a little more of Morse's past. Susan Fallon never expected to see Morse again. But after her husband dies she meets Morse in the police station and is so shocked she faints. She realizes she still has feelings for Morse. But then it doesn't work out between them for a second time, I'm afraid. It was a complicated, emotional part on many levels. John was wonderful to work with. Coincidentally, the last time John and I had worked together before was about the same length of time Morse and Susan Fallon had been apart, some twenty years or so. It was in the sixties when he directed a play called *Little Malcolm and His Struggle Against the Eunuchs*. It was a small-budget production in which I was the only woman.

'All actors long to be in *Morse* because it is so wonderfully written and beautifully acted. To tell the truth I was terrified of letting the side down. John is totally professional. You couldn't ask for a more perfect acting partner. You have to remember he is under tremendous pressure. He has to carry *Inspector Morse* and has a massive amount of dialogue to learn. But he always knows his lines and he expects you to know yours. When he is around everyone has to come up to scratch.'

John always paid tribute to pioneering producer Kenny McBain, the driving force behind getting *Inspector Morse* off the ground in the first place. 'Kenny was right about so many things,' said John. 'He wanted each *Morse* story to be a film in its own right and I agree. I like the idea that people switch on without knowing exactly what they're going to get. People are intrigued by the solitary nature of Morse.

'We have had some good times with *Morse* but we had some sad times as well. The saddest thing about it is that Ken died so young. In a way it was Ken who created Morse. He was the man who had the idea to film Colin Dexter's Morse books. He was the original producer who cast me, got the writers together, brought in the designer, and put our team together. He always insisted on the very highest quality. Ken was a very, very clever, bright intelligent fellow. He was only thirty-seven when he died.'

Thaw believes passionately in the quality of the production of *Morse*. 'I always want the best of everything: writers, actors, technicians, everything. I believe *Morse* proves that if you give people a quality product then they'll watch. What they won't watch is cheap stuff which is made for threepence ha'penny masquerading as innovative drama. Sam Goldwyn said that no one ever went broke underestimating the taste of the public but I believe the precise opposite of that. I believe people deserve the best and that they appreciate quality and I think *Inspector Morse* helps to prove that.

'Occasionally in *Morse* we get what we could politely describe as not very speakable lines and I think, "If I say this the way it's written either they're going to laugh or they're going to turn off." So I try to find a way that keeps people interested. I might leave a pause where no rational person would leave a pause. Or say it quickly where no rational person would say it quickly. Things like that. It's breaking the rules. I know it's not real but whoever said *Morse* was real?'

In a famous exchange Lewis said: 'Morse's Law is that "The person who discovers the body is often the murderer." ' But Morse insists that his law is quite different: 'Morse's Law is that there's always time for one more pint,' he almost chortles, and sends Lewis scuttling to the bar. It is the sort of delicious *Morse* moment which John Thaw delivers so brilliantly. Yet he insists years of playing the character have done nothing to improve his own powers of detection. Thaw admits he frequently finds it difficult to work out who is the guilty man or woman. He says: 'Even when I am reading my own script when it comes to the crunch I am always surprised to find out who is really guilty.'

For series six, filmed in the summer of 1991, there was yet another unforgettable *Morse* highlight with an investigation that took Morse and the ever faithful Lewis to sun-soaked Italy. After the wettest June on record in Oxford the travelling circus of some twenty large trucks and just over a hundred cast and crew moved to the sweltering city of Verona and temperatures of over 100 degrees Fahrenheit. This time both John Thaw and Inspector Morse approved of the trip.

But before filming in Italy, John and Sheila enjoyed a holiday in the south of France. 'We went to Provence before I started this *Morse* series, whenever it was. I've lost all track of time now. And we spent a week driving around and eating. We seemed to go from restaurant to restaurant and of course I came back about half a stone heavier than when I went. Not that I am bothered that much. I think it's quite Morse-like really for him to have a little bit of a tummy on him. That's my excuse and I'm sticking to it.

'*Morse* in Italy is a mirror image of the Australian film, where you had Morse as the grumpy one who didn't like it and Lewis took to it like a duck to water. In Italy it was the reverse, Morse really loves it and Lewis wants to get home. Morse loves the food, the wine, the music and the love of life of the Italians. Lewis can't speak the language so he can't understand what people are saying. He just wants to get home to his wife and kids.

'*Morse* in Australia was very different. For my money it succeeded because it was so different. There was some great team work. Morse and I agree on Italy. We both like Italians and their painting and their food and particularly their music. I had a great time working there with my scallywags. I love the things people say. One of the crew said very seriously that he was hoping to take a look at Pisa while he was in Italy. Only he pronounced it like Pizza.

'And the wife of one of the drivers came over during filming and went into Venice shopping one morning. I was surprised to see her back by lunchtime. I asked her if she liked it, and she looked at me and said, "Yes, but it's a bit repetitive." I almost choked on my lunch. I said, "Did you see St Mark's Square," and she said, "I suppose I must have done. I walked everywhere." She had been round a few shops and somehow never saw the beautiful canals and the amazing buildings.

'People really amuse me sometimes. Mind you, they're not always flattering. I've always looked older than my years and I think I was forty-eight when one of the crew said to my driver, "Our John is not bad for his age is he?" My driver asked, "How old do you think he is?" And the answer came back, "Well, he's got to be fifty-eight, hasn't he?" ' said John with a roar of laughter. 'I went grey early. It really happened while we were filming *The Sweeney*. In fact if you watch all the episodes you'll see me gradually going. And just after *The Sweeney* I went totally white. It's

French leave: on the set of *A Year in Provence* and with his co-star Lindsay Duncan. (Scope Features)

Above and left: John with Inspector Morse's beloved Jaguar and with his co-star Kevin Whately.
(Rex Features, Scope Features)

Top right: Brought to book: the two Morse stars with author Colin Dexter.
(All Action)

Right: John and Kevin in formal attire at an awards function.
(Rex Features)

Above: Award winner: John with proud wife, Sheila Hancock. (Rex Features)

Left: John and Sheila on the steps of Number 10 Downing Street. (Rex Features)

Above: Outside
Buckingham Palace with
his CBE.
(Express Newspapers)

Right: John with
another TV sleuth,
Angela Lansbury of
Murder She Wrote.
(Rex Features)

Family man: John with Sheila and the children. (Rex Features)

John and Sheila have been married for nearly twenty five years. Here is the doting dad with one of his children.
(All Action, Scope Features)

John relaxing at his Chiswick home
and in his study there.
(Scope Features)

a hereditary thing. My father went white when he was about twenty-five.'

He was friendly to actors up to a point but John Thaw was definitely not a 'luvvie'. Between takes, he found it very hard to talk to other actors about anything but work. He was certainly not one to make polite conversation and never found it easy to talk about what he did because he joked that he was not quite sure what it was himself. He found it hard to talk about himself and would much rather sit in silence, or better still listening to some of his classical music, rather than make small talk. He hated parties where he felt 'under surveillance'.

The Italian *Morse* adventure was written by Alma Cullen and called 'The Death of the Self'. Morse and Lewis travelled to the Veneto to investigate the death of an Englishwoman who was attending an expensive psychotherapy course near Vicenza. The other patients attending the course were questioned and they included Nicole Burgess, a well-known opera singer whose career has collapsed following a nervous breakdown. Already a great fan of her work, Morse is enchanted by the glamorous Nicole, played by Frances Barber, and goes to see her rehearse at the great Roman Arena in Verona, where she is planning to make her comeback during the famous Opera Festival.

'It isn't a flirtation,' insisted John on location, even though he was filming in the city where *Romeo and Juliet* was set. 'He has her records at home and he is a huge fan so when he meets her he is starstruck and for a time completely bowled over. But in the story she has not sung for a few years. She is a heroine to Morse but he feels admiration and deep respect for her rather than anything stronger or long-lasting. She is married and I don't think

Morse would ever get really involved with a married woman. I know in the story she is not very happily married but Morse still would not get involved.'

Frances Barber was certainly enthusiastic about her role. She said: 'I got to do what millions of housewives all over the world want to do – kiss Inspector Morse. My character has this passionate thing with Morse. I didn't think it shocked Morse fans but hopefully it excited them. It's a wonderful part, very emotional. I got to sing an aria from *Turandot* at the Verona Opera Festival and not many actresses will be able to say that. Actually I was miming and the voice came from opera singer Janis Kelly but it took a lot of hard training to get the breathing right. I can sing, but not that well. Working with John Thaw was wonderful. John was exactly as I expected him to be, an absolute gent, a great delight and very exciting.'

John enjoyed it too, but he and producer Deirdre Keir were careful not to make the film too shocking. He said: 'We had a body impaled on a spike in the Italian story but we didn't want the viewers to see the thing protruding through a woman's neck. You can't have too much blood and gore because they go out at eight o'clock, well before the watershed. But we've never had that anyway in *Morse*. We don't need it. We can suggest death by people's reactions or cut to a pair of feet on the floor to show that somebody's dead. We don't want to see her up on a spike with blood pouring out of her earholes. Nobody wants to see that.

'There were some really magical scenes in the Italian *Morse*. We filmed during Gala Night at the opera when even the cheap seats cost a hundred pounds and some go for a thousand. There were twenty-five thousand people in the audience and some of them had booked ten years before. There was me and Kev in among all the candles and they didn't take any notice. They care about opera over there, not about two blokes from England pretending to be policemen.

'Her character sang *Turandot* which has always been one of my favourites. And it was wonderful to have Sheila sitting behind me in the audience. She had some time off and as we both love Italy she came over for a brief holiday. The opera was such a marvellous spectacle I thought she should be in on it.'

The effect on screen was stunning but the recording of the big day was one of the most difficult in *Morse* history. Crew and actors were working all day in the exposed basin of the Arena, where the temperature is reckoned to be seven degrees higher than outside, and long into the night for Frances Barber to mime to the famous aria.

On the day she admitted she was terrified, but before the schedule even reached her big moment and she stepped on to the stage trodden by opera stars from Caruso to Callas to Carreras, there was twelve hours of exhausting filming to conclude. By midday the temperature had soared to 110 degrees and the glare from the white marble of the Arena was dazzling. '*Lawrence of Arabia* wasn't as hot as this,' muttered one veteran member of the crew.

As the make-up department struggled to keep John Thaw looking cool it was Kevin Whately who landed the worst task of the day, sprinting the length of Verona's main square in hot pursuit of a suspect. As the pavements sizzled and the tourists took refuge in shady cafés the only movement in the square was from the gently fluttering flags which decorate the town in high season. A voice from high at the top of the Arena yelled 'Action' and Kevin rushed across the square, some eight times to ensure an acceptable take. Then as the light of the evening began to fade Frances Barber prepared for her ordeal. She had watched a performance of Puccini's *Turandot* the night before in the Arena. The largest open-air theatre in the world, it was built more than 2,000 years ago when it was second only in size and importance to the Colosseum in Rome. The Arena was originally used by the Romans for gladiator fighting and bloodsports but now it is famous for its annual opera festival which, since 1913, has attracted the world's greatest opera singers.

It was here that Maria Callas, after years of frustration and disappointment, appeared in *La Gioconda* in 1947 and was first brought to the attention of the world. Frances wasn't quite that good but when it reached transmission this stunning spectacle made for a breathtaking *Inspector Morse* film. It remained one of John Thaw's favourites.

By 1992 John Thaw said publicly what he had often said privately – that after six years of success with *Inspector Morse* it was perhaps time to stop and move on to new projects. He explained: 'I am going to do one more series and that's the end. I have gone as far as I can with the character. Dare I say I think it's still good. I think the series we are doing now is as good as anything we have done before. But you get to the stage where it's time to stop. Just as we did with *The Sweeney* you have to know when to stop. If it were left to Thames TV we would still be making it, in fact with all the repeats it looks as though we *are* still making it. You just get to the stage where everyone – the actors, the writers and the directors – thinks, "Well, it's still good, but it's just a little harder to come up with a fresh enough story." And the actors are finding it just a little harder to get out of bed at five in the morning. When you get a few days like that you start to think, "Well, maybe it's time to call it a day." People enjoy four or five *Morse*s a year so we provide them, but they would get pretty fed-up if the quality fell off, as, with the best will in the world, it will eventually. You'll see the same stories being reworked and then it will be "Hang on a minute, haven't I seen this before?" '

Thaw admitted to a tinge of melancholy over Morse's demise. 'I feel a mixture of delight and sadness at his passing, as I've lived with the fellow all these years. But I'm glad it's coming to an end because it's getting harder to bring something new to each film, which was always our aim.

'But policemen do retire in their fifties and that is where I am now, so the timing is right from that point of view. I am not bored with Morse, it's just that all good things must come to an end. I don't want to go on and on being Morse for ever. There are lots of other parts I want to play. I am a professional actor. That's my job. I want to do work people want to watch, but just because some people would like more *Morse* I can't go on for ever. The idea of becoming typecast did not come into my decision at all. I never became stereotyped as Regan. I just knew it had to come to the end. We have got all we can out of it. Kevin and I chatted on the last series and we both separately came to the same conclusion.

'I never thought it would be as popular as it became. I thought it would go for two or three series at a pinch. I liked the idea of each show being two hours and I liked the character of Morse. For me it was the character that set it apart.'

As the show came to what appeared to be a final close, John Thaw paid a fond and heartfelt tribute to his long-suffering assistant when he added: 'If you ask me what I will really miss, I have to say it will be Kevin Whately. I have loved working with Kevin and the rest of the cast and crew, but I know that I'm going to be able to work with them again. The acting world is quite a small one. And Kevin is actually going to be working with my daughter Elly Jane in his new series, *Peak Practice*.

'With the end of *Morse* comes the beginning of a great rush of people trying to come up with a similar type of show. There are thousands of producers out there scurrying round trying to come up with something as successful. I don't know what made it so special. If I did I would be a very rich man. I know that it had a great deal to do with the relationship between Morse and Lewis. People liked that. There was a chemistry they could see on screen. But I also know that there was a great chemistry they couldn't actually see but could probably feel – and that is the chemistry of the people behind the scenes. Everyone there had an incredible working relationship – crew, cameramen, actors, everyone. I shall miss *Morse* and I will also miss working with the crew and the routine of coming into make-up and wardrobe and seeing the same faces.'

Working on *Morse* had taken up months of John's busy working year and it had also had a dramatic effect upon his private life. 'To some degree I have been recognized by people in the street since I did things like *The Sweeney*, but *Morse* has blown that up by huge proportions,' said John. 'So much so that I get recognized when I go to Europe and Japanese and American tourists spot me over here. You get the feeling of constantly being watched and you don't feel totally relaxed when you are aware of people. I am bothered by it but I have to be philosophical about it.'

Yet in all the discussion about the end of such a popular series John Thaw was always careful never to close the door on *Morse* too finally. He insisted he did not want Morse to die in his last investigation. 'I just want to leave him to get on with his job. I think that is what the public would prefer,' he said. 'I don't want to see him killed off because that would be very sad. And I don't think he will be. I think Colin's publisher might have something to say about that.'

Julian Mitchell wrote what was then described as the last *Morse*, a memorable story called 'Twilight of the Gods' which featured devoted *Morse* fan Sir John Gielgud as a highly eccentric Chancellor of Oxford University and Robert Hardy as an unscrupulous tycoon closely modelled on Robert Maxwell.

The newspapers of the day were full of inaccurate reports that Morse died in a hail of gunfire as the final credits rolled. Julian said: 'I was certainly not allowed to kill off Morse, nor would I have wanted to end with that sort of bang. But I think *Morse* fans enjoyed the last story. It was full of Morse's favourite Wagner music. Sir John's character was presiding over a grand ceremony giving honorary degrees to a Welsh opera singer played by Sheila Gish and to Robert Hardy's tycoon. Suddenly, as they are walking through the streets in their gladrags in this great procession, a shot rings out and someone falls dead.' But it was most certainly not Inspector Morse. Mitchell has watched Thaw deliver mesmeric performances for years and clearly recognizes the actor as 'brilliant' but remains uncertain as to what made him the consummate television actor. The writer said: 'If anyone knew then everyone would imitate him. His technique is perfect and by seeming to do very little he conveys so much.'

John celebrated the final day of filming in a way his screen character would most emphatically have approved of – with a drink. 'There were definitely no major dramatics when we finished filming,' he said. 'We stopped shooting, had a drink or two and then I got into a chauffeur-driven Jaguar and I was taken home – probably half-cut. I will miss Morse but, while one half of me was quite sad, I also felt quite happy that it was all finished.'

And, prophetically, he refused to rule out a possible Morse return one day. 'I would never say Morse must never darken my doorstep again, but in the foreseeable future it's over. Sheila thought it was a good idea to quit while you're ahead but she did not influence my decision.' And significantly he added: 'If they come up with a brilliant idea for a one-off *Morse* in two or three years then I will consider it in the same way I would consider any film offer. But a series? No.'

As a change of gear from melancholy Morse, John Thaw was persuaded to star in a four-part adaptation of Kingsley Amis's controversial novel *Stanley and the Women*. The project was first suggested to Thaw in 1988 and finally got under way in 1991. The story centres on the plight of Stanley West, whose idyllic lifestyle is shattered when his son develops a terrifying mental illness. As Stanley struggles to help his son regain his sanity he finds himself locked in a harrowing battle with the medical profession in general, and a monstrous lady psychiatrist in particular. His beautiful, cultured second wife and her more strident predecessor turn out to be no help at all in a traumatic and heart-rending human dilemma.

John Thaw was irritated when the project was announced because the book was misrepresented in the press. He was quick to make an important point. 'It's not boozing, bonking Stanley, it's really not. It's just a clever title that has sold Kingsley Amis some books. It was the first Kingsley Amis book I had ever read and it is still the only Kingsley Amis book I have ever read. I agree with his son Martin Amis who said, "My father doesn't use enough commas." I had to keep re-reading bits and I found I was reading the book twice in one go. The female characters were mainly less than sympathetic and when the book was published in America the powerful Women's Movement was so angered by what they called "the negative portrayal of women" they attempted to get it banned.'

Thaw went to great lengths to make newspaperman Stanley as different as possible from policeman Morse. And his distinguished grey hair was dyed to what Sheila described as 'a terrible shade of orange'.

But the star was determined. 'I hope the difference between Morse and Stanley is pretty large,' said John Thaw, relaxing in his caravan as filming started. 'Otherwise I might have to re-think my career.' He added, 'Laurence Olivier's advice about amazing myself with my own daring came back to me as I began work on *Stanley* and I think as I have got older I have tried to become bolder. I now attempt to do things about which I think to myself beforehand, "If this doesn't work you're going to look a real prat." When you're a young actor you sometimes don't want to do things because you don't want to look a prat. As you get older you don't care so much. You think, "So what if I look a prat?"

'I was pleased to be asked to play the part. It keeps the batteries recharged to do something so completely different. I think it is quite a brave and enterprising move by Central TV because it is not an obvious ratings grabber.

'I hope it will be another example of how it is possible to make high-quality television which attracts high ratings. It is being made by a lot of the people who make *Morse*, the finest technicians and a wonderful cast. The basic story is a very good tale. As in *Morse,* I think that is what people want. They like to see good stories and they like to see them well acted and well made. And because of that I think *Stanley* will work and people will watch and enjoy it. People are not mugs. If you make something for three-pence ha'penny and say, "Here you are, spend an hour watching this," they are not going to be fooled. They are going to look at it and say, "This isn't good." '

As mentioned, Kingsley Amis's style did not at first appeal to Thaw. 'The book is somewhat alarming,' he said. 'I didn't like it at all and a lot of changes were made. We softened the characters and some of the more caustic style came out naturally. It's obvious when you read it that a lot of Amis's so-called anti-feminist views are on the page as Stanley's thoughts. Obviously you can't do that in a script, so when that is stripped away and you are left with Amis's bare dialogue, and the dialogue added by Nigel Kneale, then it became much more my cup of tea. When real-live actresses started playing the parts of The Women that soft-ened Amis's original still further. That was no bad thing. If we had played it like the book it would have been totally unbelievable. Some people call it a black comedy but I thought at first it was more of a bleak comedy. People whose opinion I respect rush out and buy the new Amis, but he is not one of my favourites. It's a tragic story. There are a lot of very funny things in it but they come out of very, very tragic situations. But as David Tucker the direc-tor and I were saying, that is what happens in life.

'When her first husband died my wife Sheila went with a male friend to register the death to the Registrar of Births, Marriages and Deaths in Hammersmith. And the guy came out and said, "Are you the happy couple?" That was funny and they had to laugh. But the poor guy who thought they were there to get married was very upset. Laughter can come out of tragedy. Sometimes people laugh at things to help them survive them.

'Psychiatrists don't come out of *Stanley* too well. But since the book was written a lot more research has been done and now a lot of members of the psychiatric profession would think Stanley was right and that the psychiatrist was not doing things right. These days I think most of the medical profession would agree with Amis's point of view. But comedy can come out of tragedy as a sort of release. Humour does come from dreadful situations so I hope some laughter will come out of that blackness. Otherwise we're in for a very turgid four hours.

'I didn't enjoy reading the book but I did very much enjoy reading the scripts,' Thaw told one of the authors. Then, visibly remembering he was speaking to a journalist, he added: 'Maybe if I read it again I would feel differently. I am just being honest, I don't know whether I should be really but that is the truth. Initially reading the book put me off but I loved the scripts and that is why I agreed to play the part. Plus, of course, because the role is so very different to Morse. Stanley is the opposite of Morse in just about every way, so that was a big attraction for me.'

The ambitious project did test Thaw's acting abilities to the full and he explained some of the stresses that go with the job. 'Acting on television or in films can be bloody hard work. Sometimes you have to recreate the same emotion thirty times and you start to think, "Christ, where am I going to get some more emotion from?" And part of the frustration can be that each time you have to do it is because something that is nothing to do with you has gone wrong. Each time it has to be as good as the other thirty times because that could be the one they will use. And sometimes all because some silly man with a microphone has got in shot I've got to do it again. It's just pure concentration. There was one scene in *Stanley* where he breaks down and cries from nothing. It's a long scene where he starts by slowly shaking, then starts to cry and eventually becomes completely distraught. We did that five times and each time I had to use all my training and experience to generate that emotion. Concentrating that hard is very draining.

'But at the end of a scene I do come out of it straight away. I know some actors stay in character throughout a production but I would go potty if I tried that. I just immediately think, "I've got to have a cup of tea." And when I've done a scene it is wiped out straight away. If I have to do it again I have to start from scratch again. On *Stanley* we had a nine-week shoot and afterwards there was one long scene I had with an actress in a kitchen that had to be reshot. When we went back and did it again I felt I had never done it in the first place. It was really weird because even though it was a two and a half-minute scene I really do just blank out everything I have done.'

Filming the series brought much interest from the public as Thaw's character had to drive an expensive Jensen Interceptor. 'Some people seemed to think old Morse had had a pay rise,' said the actor wryly.

'*Stanley* is traumatic but it's only acting. Only pretending. I can get very involved, like in the very intense scenes with Sam West who played my deeply disturbed son. But then I can switch off. I know I'm lucky that I can switch off.'

The late Kingsley Amis was consulted at the time about the production but offered very little advice or guidance. John Thaw noted: 'He's at the sort of age now where he doesn't give a bugger for anyone. He shows no interest in *Stanley*. Mind you, politically that's a very good position for him to take because if it's a success he'll sell more books and if it's a failure he'll say, "It's nothing to do with me." '

There were some deeply harrowing scenes in *Stanley*, not least when Thaw has to stand in pouring rain desperately trying to coax his disturbed son down from a tree. Despite a morning spent getting drenched Thaw still raised a smile when his long-serving minder John Allen quickly covered him in a dressing gown and mutters, 'You'll kill him in the next round.'

John said: 'Stanley does seem like a nice guy surrounded by a lot of dreadful women. I'm sure that was Amis's intention. But in the scripts the women are not as Amazonian as they are in his book. They are much more human. And we have good actresses playing them. They are certainly not such monsters as he has them in the book. For my money that attitude to women seems misogynistic to me and I don't like that. Particularly as my family comprises a wife and three daughters. I can't identify with some of the characters in the book. I'm sure Kingsley would say there are women that appalling and even take you to meet some, because I'm told he basically writes about people he knows.'

9

A YEAR IN PROVENCE

It could have been an idyllic spring and summer for John
Thaw and Sheila Hancock. So frequently separated by
work, the couple now appeared to have a unique chance
not only to co-star together in an important new television
series, but to film it almost on the doorstep of a house they
had bought in France.

The project was *A Year in Provence*, an adaptation of a
hugely popular book by former advertising executive
Peter Mayle who had upped from England with his wife
Jennie to the Provence region of France, intending to write
a novel. Instead he'd written a delightful account of his
new life doing up an old farmhouse they had bought in the
Luberon National Park.

For John and Sheila the project could hardly have been
more appealing – some fifteen weeks in one of the most
scenic and unspoilt areas of France, starring roles in an
adaptation of a best-seller, and going home each night after
filming to their own home.

In recession-hit Britain Mayle's tale of Gallic escapism
with its lyrical, garlic-scented descriptions of fine food and
wines and his amusing accounts of the vagaries of the
locals, the goat races, and the DIY bodging of the French

174

builders struck a timely chord and swept *A Year in Provence* to the top of the best-seller lists. The book's universally appealing theme of escaping the rat-race and living the dream ensured that paperback sales worldwide comfortably topped 1 million.

Mayle had spent fifteen years in the advertising business, first as a copywriter and then as a reluctant executive before escaping Madison Avenue in New York in 1975 to write books.

For some eighteen years he and Jennie had been enthusiastic visitors to Provence. Most years they had travelled to the region at least once, often twice and more frequently when the opportunity had arisen. 'We always loved it, always felt reluctant to leave and always said what we'd really love was a house of our own down there one day,' Mayle reflected. 'Then we got to the stage where we thought if we didn't do it fairly soon we'd be that couple still sitting there talking about it.'

The Mayles owned a house in Devon but increasingly wished they were in Provence, especially when winter began to take its annual grey grip on the West Country. 'We used to sit in Devon which is fabulous – but it's wet,' said Mayle. 'I love light and I used to sit there in the winter and tell myself there must be another place to do my job, which is writing.'

One autumn on yet another trip to Provence they spied the house outside the village of Menerbes which was to change their lives so dramatically. 'Among the vines,' Mayle was to write in *A Year in Provence*, 'stood an old farmhouse, weathered by wind and sun to a colour somewhere between honey and pale grey. In the afternoon sun, with the wooden shutters half closed like sleepy eyelids, it was irresistible . . .'

To such an extent that the Mayles decided on the spot to buy it. 'We hadn't got any money at that time,' Mayle recalled, 'but we did have the house in Devon so we shook hands on it, had a drink then rushed back to England thinking, "Christ, how are we going to pay for it?" We had to sell the Devon house and take a chance. We had no idea what sort of people we'd be living with.

'Although I didn't have an idea for a novel I'd decided I was going to write one and I thought a house in Provence would mean no interruptions, no distractions, tranquil, calm, and nice weather. I thought that's what a writer ought to do. But I'm not a country boy at heart and that's what's so strange. I lived in and was born in London, worked in London and New York and I don't think I got my shoes wet until I was thirty. It really was a huge transformation.'

Once renovations began on the house, Mayle found it difficult even to think, let alone write amid the constant din and toing and froing of men at work. 'It was impossible to concentrate for two reasons,' he said. 'Firstly, there was a real physical danger because the house really was being knocked about in a big way. Secondly, if I happened to be sitting there with a typewriter then I kept being told to move. I found myself playing hide and seek with the workmen as I dodged about the house but gradually I became more and more fascinated with what they did, how they did it and the way they behaved to each other; the fact that they started at seven in the morning and ate a proper lunch – banal to Frenchmen but new to us.

'As far as any writing went, all I was doing was writing letters to my agent saying, "I'm terribly sorry I haven't started the novel yet because all this has been happening," and I went on to explain all the changes to the house.

Eventually he asked whether I'd ever thought of putting it all down in a coherent form. I said I didn't think anyone would be interested because knocking down walls and getting your pipes fixed isn't instantly the most promising material in literature. But he said he knew a publisher in London which was very Francophile; they might just be interested and why didn't I write a synopsis and a specimen ten pages? That's when I really started watching and observing the workmen coming and going and I duly wrote a synopsis and first chapter and I got a call saying they were prepared to publish it.

'I spent the next six months writing and I thought *A Year in Provence* would be published as a souvenir of a very important change in one's life. That's all. To be honest, I never envisaged it as a book, let alone a television series – I didn't think it would do better than get published and maybe I could use it as personal Christmas presents.

'It came out very modestly in London and they printed three thousand copies but it in no way meant that I could retire and buy a racehorse. Then, after a month, they said they were going to reprint and they reprinted and reprinted and then came the paperback and suddenly we started finding people coming up the drive with a copy of the book saying: "Can you sign this and where can we eat lunch?"

'It must have been some fluke of timing when the paperback came out or people read it and liked the fact it didn't have someone getting shot or maimed or having sex every thirteen pages. It clearly touched some kind of nerve in the public which I'm very grateful for, because it certainly wasn't deliberate or anything that was expected. It's a fairly simple account of an Englishman's reaction to his new life in France and the book was written more for love than for money in the beginning. It's very nice to have an honest enthusiasm which has no commercial motive.'

Finding the dream house was only the start of the Mayles' Provençal adventure – and their problems. In Peter's book the difficulties start in February when they hired an army of French workmen to renovate the house and by June the jobs were still unfinished. But the bonuses of meeting Gallic characters galore and the epicurean feasts they were able to enjoy captured the public's imagination and kept *A Year in Provence* at the top of the best-seller lists for many months.

On the back of the book's success, other commercial possibilities presented themselves for *A Year in Provence*. Mayle himself read it on the radio – and among the enthusiastic listeners was John Thaw. Mayle also read the book himself for audio cassette and there was considerable interest in the film and TV rights.

To the movie moguls of Hollywood, it all looked so ridiculously simple. They had it all planned – buy up the film rights to Peter Mayle's runaway best-seller, instal Richard Chamberlain and Meryl Streep, two of the screen's hottest, most glamorous and bankable stars, in the lead roles, take the whole movie-making circus to the south of France and cash in.

What they had not bargained for was Barry Hanson, then head of drama at Pebble Mill, the BBC's Birmingham studios. While the Hollywood moviemen were punching their calculators and doing their sums over their morning melon, Mayle was sitting down to discuss the TV rights with Hanson, who in his time had been responsible for such acclaimed productions as *The Naked Civil Servant* and *The Long Good Friday*.

ITV was also interested in bringing *A Year in Provence* to

the screen but, after the BBC's initial approach, Hanson enterprisingly arrived on the doorstep of Peter and Jennie Mayle's home tucked between the two medieval hill villages of Menerbes and Bonnieux. As soon as the couple opened the door to find Hanson standing there wearing a straw hat and shorts with a sunburned face and peeling nose, they immediately warmed to his infectious enthusiasm.

Over a glass of Mayle's own Côtes du Luberon wine, the suave former advertising executive and the BBC drama boss talked business and the Americans found the project grabbed right from under their noses. Mayle sold the rights to the BBC.

'There was an American network who were interested in turning *A Year in Provence* into a two-hour special with Meryl Streep and Richard Chamberlain,' says Mayle who, with his tall, slim, fair-haired good looks, bears more than a passing resemblance to Chamberlain. 'But you could just see those two treading the vines, couldn't you?' He laughed. 'It was flattering, but we weren't too keen. When the BBC offer came through, they didn't just call up and say: "Hey! Guess what, kid?" in the American way. There was just a polite note saying: "We are considering aspects of your work, would you be agreeable etc., yours sincerely." I liked that. It was no momentous event – the most exciting thing was seeing Barry Hanson turn up in his shorts!'

John Thaw, fresh from enthralling the nation with *Inspector Morse*, was chosen to play Peter Mayle. In his bestseller Mayle never mentions his wife by name and in fact the only time her name appears is in the dedication at the front of the book: 'To Jennie with love and thanks.' But to sustain a twelve-part drama series it was patently clear that Mayle's wife had to become a major character.

Scriptwriter Michael Sadler was given the task of specially creating the role of 'Annie'. He had been an obvious choice because he was married to a Frenchwoman, had lived in France for several years, had a house in the Loire Valley and was principal lecturer at the Institute Britannique in Paris, specializing in drama.

With John Thaw in place, Sheila Hancock was approached to play the role of Annie. What better choice could there be, considering she was John's wife? It was felt that viewers would be intrigued to see them together, enjoying Provençal life. But the director, who was appointed *after* Sheila had been approached, thought differently. He took the decision it would be better if Mayle's wife was played by an actress who was a good deal younger than the husband even though, as Sheila was quick to point out, nothing in the script demanded she should be.

It was a decision which inevitably caused huge repercussions and put John in an invidious position. When the news broke that Sheila had not been given the role, John must have been seething inwardly but tactfully he just expressed 'anger and disappointment' and said he was very surprised Sheila wasn't now to play his wife. The BBC, desperate not to inflame the situation, delicately confirmed that Sheila had indeed been considered for the part 'but she just wasn't right'. Then a member of the production team said bluntly: 'Sheila was probably thought too old for the role and not glamorous enough. The Mayles, after all, were starting a new life in Provence. They're not supposed to look as if they are in a retirement home.'

That provoked a swift reaction from Sheila. 'The funny thing is that I'm OK as John's wife in real life,' she said, 'but suddenly I'm unsuitable to be his wife on television. That is ludicrous. I suppose they want somebody who looks more dolly-birdish. But why? It's a male concept and it's awfully sad.

'They may be justified in saying I'm not glamorous enough but I wasn't aware that it was supposed to be a frightfully glamorous part. John is not exactly Peter Mayle so they aren't casting it true to the book in any case.'

Sheila went on to express publicly the opinion that her role had been sacrificed on the altar of men's middle-aged fantasies. 'The people who make the decisions on what should be done are men. It's just ageism and sexism,' she reasoned. 'But if these nasty little creatures think we're only ready for the retirement home we really are in trouble.'

Soon afterwards Lindsay Duncan, blonde, undeniably pretty and a youthful-looking forty-two had the delicate task of slipping into the role earmarked for Sheila opposite Sheila's husband.

Losing the role of Annie also meant for Sheila that she and John could not look forward to their fifteen weeks together staying at their own farmhouse for the duration of filming. They genuinely shared Mayle's love of Provence because even before the remarkable success of Mayle's book, the couple had bought their own particular slice of privacy in what remains one of the last untouched, tranquil areas of paradise in Europe.

The possibility of having a second home in France had often crossed their minds and they decided to buy in Provence after Melanie had taken a part in an episode of *Bergerac* set in Aix en Provence near the Luberon Valley, the area north of Marseilles and east of Avignon which Peter Mayle has made so famous. Sheila went out to see Melanie while she was filming and the two of them had a short holiday and were captivated by the region's beauty with its olive groves, its glorious lavender fields carpeting the hillsides, its ancient villages and its spectacular valley views bathed in the dappled light so delightfully peculiar to the area. Sheila came back enthusing about Provence to such a degree that she emphatically told John that they simply had to have a home there, even if it was further south in France than they had originally planned.

John said: 'We knew an English couple, ironically they're social workers from Oxford, who lived there permanently with their children and we just happened to say casually to them that if anything suitable came up near by would they let us know. A week later they were on the phone to say there was a house for sale up the road.

'We drove down and when we got to the area I found it was staggeringly beautiful. All the hills and vineyards and the little hilltop villages were so attractive and I was struck by the famous Provençal light which is why all the artists came down that way. It is quite true, it is a magical light, particularly near to dusk when the colours seem to be heightened. They're not just green; they are ten shades of green, yellows and ochres.'

The house they saw was one of four converted and renovated farm buildings huddled together in a hillside hollow in the tiny hamlet of Les Gavots near the village of Saignon, about one and half hours' drive from Marseille airport. It had a magnificent view across a valley to the nearest large town of Apt, and the nearest village, Saignon, which dates back to the fourteenth century, hovers on a rocky hilltop above. Because Saignon had no shops, it attracted only people like the Thaws who were simply entranced by the sheer beauty of the region.

When they looked over the three-bedroom property it turned out to be very much what John and Sheila had been looking for. They had wanted something private but not isolated, a house roomy enough for their family but not too big to be unmanageable, and they hoped for a garden rather than the acres of field which commonly accompanied such farmhouses in the area.

'It was all a bit of a tall order,' said John, 'especially as I also wanted a house which, unlike the Mayles' house, we didn't have to start rebuilding. I didn't want to get involved in any of that Peter Mayle stuff for real. We liked the house straight away and all we needed to do was a bit of plastering and painting. We put in a new bathroom and a bit of plaster on the cracks and had it painted inside and the shutters outside and basically that was all.'

John and Sheila both saw their new property as a second home rather than a holiday home to be visited on rare occasions. With its pale stone walls, terracotta roof, salmon-pink shutters and small flagstoned terrace it was homely rather than ostentatious and far from grand. An old farm shed at the end of a roughly laid tarmac track served as a garage and the garden was not big enough for a swimming pool.

Crucially it offered the kind of privacy so precious to John yet it was in reach of neighbours in case of emergency. Situated in such a small hamlet the house was hard to find for any star-spotting tourists. It was unseen from the tiny road, screened from prying eyes by unkempt trees. Understandably, John did not relish his newly acquired home becoming yet another stop on the map for the tourists, in the way that Peter Mayle's own home had been in danger of becoming. On more than one occasion Mayle had found himself dripping wet, dressed in only a towel, after stepping from the shower to sign books for tourists who had turned up out of the blue after diligently tracking down 'The English Ecrevisse' from clues in his best-seller. It was, Mayle confessed, flattering in its own way but less than wonderful to find an inquisitive reader on his doorstep with tongue hanging out hoping for a glass or two with the author.

'I like the privacy,' said John. 'The people are country people who keep themselves to themselves and they take you as they find you, whether you're English, Swiss, French, Dutch or whatever. They take you on your own value. If there's a problem, the neighbours are there, yet they leave you totally alone and don't want to know about your life. Another reason we came here was that I'm not known here. It's a wonderful experience to go to the supermarket and not be stared at.'

John and Sheila owned a house in the Cotswolds for a few years. 'But compared with Provence it was like having a place on Piccadilly,' he said. 'In Provence I'm totally left alone. People don't want to know about my life and there's a wonderful freedom for me here. For all they know I could be the coalman. All anybody knows about me is that I'm English. If I want to walk about in shorts or a silly shirt, no one is going to point or ask to take a picture.'

John had read *A Year in Provence* soon after it came out. 'Obviously we knew the area of the Luberon and out of interest we wanted to read what the author said about it,' he said. 'It was totally the Provence I knew, totally believable, even the characters. I loved it. It was a joy to read and I immediately read it straight through.'

The practicalities of bringing *A Year in Provence* to the screen proved as tricky as the casting. Peter and Jennie Mayle wisely felt their home should not be used for the filming. Having written a best-seller highlighting the diffi-culties of doing up a house in a foreign land, Mayle was not about to have his now thoroughly ordered life and home disrupted by film crews for three months.

Instead, designer Amanda Atkinson scoured the French countryside for four months looking for the perfect home. She viewed more than eighty properties before settling on a huge farmhouse some ten kilometres from the Mayles', off the road between Bonnieux and Rousillon, which satis-fied her specific requirements. It was brimming with character, enjoyed magnificent views of the Luberon Valley and the mountains beyond and was big enough to hold a TV crew. It also had a swimming pool which saved the BBC from having to have one built. It belonged to a wealthy Parisian, the proprietor of the Paris air show, and his wife, and the BBC negotiated to rent it for £600 a week.

A dozen workmen spent £17,000 and almost a month transforming the chic holiday home into an old weather-beaten farmhouse as near in detail as possible to Peter Mayle's real home. The exterior was coated four times with layers of pigment, including one skin of black latex, to make it look old, and when filming finished the BBC simply had to remove the coverings to restore the house to its original look.

Inside, much of the furniture was stacked up, taken away in a removal van and put into storage. 'The owner popped down from Paris to keep an eye on what was going on,' said Amanda. 'He seemed to like the changes we made. But, even so, we guaranteed to restore the prop-erty to pristine condition and in the end he was more than delighted when we handed it back.'

By the time the builders, carpenters and artists had finished, the glorious farmhouse designed to sell Peter

Mayle's dream to millions of TV viewers was an extraordinary fake. Even the tumbling wisteria was false. Although the actual plant was genuine, more than a hundred tiny mauve flowers and silk leaves were glued on by hand to the bush to create the right effect.

Sheds and barbecues were created from latex and polystyrene and an entire vegetable garden appeared overnight. But freak weather conditions caused huge problems. Flooding in the fields prompted the local farmers to pick their grapes just days before the BBC needed a scene with the vineyards flush with the fruit. The design team were forced to paint dozens of bunches of plastic grapes the correct light red colour and tie them on to the vines.

John Thaw and Peter Mayle had dinner a couple of times before filming began and Mayle cordially passed on a few tips about broken pipes and local builders. The meetings were convivial and unpressured, since John had made up his mind he was not going to study in detail Mayle's every word, movement and mannerism for his TV portrayal.

'The truth is that when I first took the job I knew I wasn't going to impersonate Peter Mayle,' said John. 'I couldn't do that because, although I'd met him a couple of times, I wouldn't know where to begin to impersonate him. I'd have to spend a lot of time watching him. So I thought I'd do it as a character near to me, John Thaw, but calling himself Peter Mayle.

'The first couple of days Peter came on set with his wife I did feel a bit self-conscious. Although I wasn't impersonating him, I was aware that here was the man whose name I had taken. It was a bit unnerving. As some of it was his life and some from the book and it did happen to him, it must have been a strange feeling for him to see it on screen.'

Mayle rarely watched television. Indeed his TV set was shut away in a cupboard and brought out only on odd occasions. But when three episodes of *A Year in Provence* were in the can Mayle was invited to view them. 'I approached the screening with tremendous trepidation,' he remembered. 'It was very odd to have one's life filmed.

'What I've seen looks ravishing. I think it will do very well. It's very strange to have your life filmed but the way it's done, it's not like two people impersonating Jennie and me. There are two actors playing parts in circumstances that have been dramatized from our experiences.'

John Thaw and everyone else involved with the production were heartened by Peter Mayle's reaction. 'He saw three episodes and to be honest I was very pleased,' said John. 'I saw the fax he sent to the production manager after he'd seen them and I must say I had a sense of relief that he had liked them. I'm glad he did because I'm sure he was dreading it just as much as anyone seeing what they had done to it. After that I relaxed more. I don't know what we we'd have done if he had said it was rubbish.'

To say that John's role in *A Year in Provence* was demanding is an understatement. He was in almost every shot and filming did not progress at the leisurely pace Provence is so famed for. John, Lindsay and the fifty-strong crew worked a ten-hour day, six days a week, with an hour off for lunch. Sunday was John's only day of rest.

Frequently John would arrive on location in the dark and leave in the dark. He'd be up at five-thirty in the morning and leave for home at eight. 'It is a bit gruelling,' he confessed. 'By the time I'd got home, had a bit of cheese and a baguette and had a look at the script I was off to bed ready to be up at five-thirty. It's certainly the most demanding role I've done for a long time. The nearest thing to it in the physical sense is *The Sweeney*. There's quite a bit of running about.

'Apart from liking the book, another reason for taking the role was it meant I could stay at my house here. I hadn't been able to get to it as much as I would have liked, so I thought it would be a great opportunity to be in my home, working in this beautiful scenery. As things have worked out I haven't been able to enjoy the area as much as I thought when I took the job because there is so little spare time. It's six days a week and I crash out on Sundays. I thought I'd be able to go to Marseille on a Sunday or spend a day in Aix, but I just couldn't do it. It is all a bit of a sob story. Here we are in Provence where people eat and drink and all we can do is crawl home.

'But I've really appreciated what little I've seen of our house. It feels like home, particularly on Sunday when I literally potter about. I don't like going away and I get particularly homesick but it is different having our house here. I can phone Sheila and she can phone me and some-how it isn't quite the same as being in the middle of a city where I feel cut off.'

To everyone's relief John's relationship with Lindsay was harmonious both on and off screen, which might not have been the case given that Sheila Hancock was initially in the frame to play Annie. 'We hadn't worked together before but we became friends very quickly,' said Lindsay, a first-time mother at forty who agreed to take the part of Annie only if she could bring along her golden-haired, blue-eyed, sixteen-month-old son Cal, her first child with her husband, actor Hilton McRae.

By the time *A Year in Provence* was due to be launched there were whispers within certain sections of the BBC that the series was not going to be the cast-iron hit that had been hoped for. In addition, there was a worrying under-current for John and the BBC to deal with, about the effect the series might have on the Provence region.

Ever since Peter Mayle's book had become a best-seller the author had regularly been forced to defend himself against accusations that his book had attracted hordes of unwanted tourists to the area. Now, argued his critics – and Mayle had more than his fair share – this offence would be compounded by the TV series.

Mayle did his best to allay any fears that the Luberon was about to be overrun by roller-skating teenagers in baseball caps looking for the nearest disco, but the TV show's possible adverse impact on the area was still a much-raised topic at the press launch of *A Year in Provence*.

Peter Mayle lent his support to the launch by making the effort to get up at four in the morning and drive to Marseille to catch a plane to Paris and then another flight to London. Both he and John Thaw assured the doubters that the series would not adversely prompt yet more tourists to the region. Both stressed that its natural beauty had remained unspoilt for hundreds of years and that there was no reason to doubt it would remain so.

By now a major press and promotional campaign for the TV series was already in place and the public's expecta-tions had been raised to such a pitch that millions were primed to tune in and allow themselves to be beguiled by the £3 million programme.

The eagerly awaited first episode was screened on BBC1 at 8.25p.m. on 26 February 1993. It was brave scheduling, given that it was thirty-five minutes into ITV's rival show *The Darling Buds of May*, which had already proved wildly popular, with every episode topping the ratings during its first series. This scheduling was always going to be a gamble. Marcus Plantin, ITV's network director and a former BBC man, was all too aware of the threat it posed to his banker show. 'We took a view to kill it,' said Plantin of *A Year in Provence*, 'absolutely kill it.'

David Jason had scored a stunning success playing lovable Pop Larkin in the glossy adaptation of the HE Bates novels about life with the Larkins in the Kent countryside in the 1950s. It was therefore asking a lot of John Thaw and *A Year in Provence* to tempt viewers away. They would have to switch channels halfway through *The Darling Buds of May*. The big question was whether *A Year in Provence* was strong enough to achieve that.

At first it appeared the BBC had pulled off a remarkable victory over ITV. The opening episode was watched by 14.5 million viewers with *The Darling Buds of May* pulling in 13.8 million, as opposed to its normal 17 million. But most newspaper critics were unimpressed, one describing it as 'an idiotic concoction of travelogue shots, condescending portraits of comical French artisans and hammed-up linguistic clumsiness'. Others complained that the television version did not capture the book's mood and that John Thaw as Peter Mayle was not shown wallowing in Provençal cuisine as often as he did in the book.

Stung by the reviews, Mark Shivas, the BBC's head of drama, called them snobbish and grudging. 'I think it rather sad that people cannot find some enjoyment out of a very civilized programme,' he retorted. 'The idea that you had to see Mayle eating all four desserts in a restaurant is rubbish. You don't want too much food on television.'

In an article in *The Times* the distinguished director Philip Saville said that he felt *A Year in Provence* needed a 'more romantic approach' and John Thaw's Peter Mayle had a 'surly disregard for life' which was not quite right for the part. He said: 'Thaw is a very fine actor but it is hard to dissociate him from Inspector Morse and the programme came unstuck because of that. I would have cast it differently and had someone more like Michael Palin or even Dudley Moore.'

The spirited defence of the show by Mark Shivas could not, however, prevent the second episode dipping by 2.5 million viewers and the third by a further 2.5 million. The fourth and fifth episodes attracted only 7.5 million and halfway through the series the figure had plunged to 6.2 million. That dismal figure produced a tie in the television ratings with *Eldorado*, the doomed BBC soap set in Spain. It was low enough for both programmes to drop out of the Top 30.

With the audience eroding so alarmingly, there could have been better and happier moments for John Thaw to arrive at Buckingham Palace to collect the CBE he had been awarded by the Queen. Apparently the Queen let it be known that she had watched John in both *Inspector Morse* and *A Year in Provence*. She said that playing a genial Englishman in France, he now appeared much different from grumpy Morse. But outside Buckingham Palace John's proud smile turned into an icy grimace when he was asked about *A Year in Provence* and its vanishing viewers. 'Obviously I'd like more people to watch it,' he said irritably. 'But I don't give a damn what the press say about it. I don't want to talk about *A Year in Provence*.'

The BBC attempted to salvage the series by screening the show earlier in the evening against Granada TV's light comedy *Watching*. A further 1 million viewers for *Watching* was the depressing outcome.

Perhaps the most wounding criticism of all came from Sue Lawley on the BBC's audience-reaction programme *Biteback* when she pronounced *A Year in Provence* 'one of the great disappointments of the current television season'.

In the glorious certainty of hindsight it is not difficult to pinpoint why *A Year in Provence* turned out to be such a disappointment. It was, after all, based on a diary where there was a distinct lack of drama and little action. There were plenty of fine meals to be eaten, goat races to be run, and French builders to bodge, but no unfolding story and no conflict to hold the viewers' attention. While the arrival of a heavy garden table might be of interest, it is hardly a gripping event. In terms of TV drama, it was asking a lot from its audience to hold their breath in excitement over something essentially so unimportant.

One of the BBC team who worked on the show expressed the general disappointment that it had turned out to be such a flop. 'It seemed to have everything going for it,' he said. 'It was adapted from a best-seller, it had an established, much admired, much liked star and it had the most gorgeous scenery you could imagine. It looked like a sure-fire hit.

'The show had been the baby of Jonathan Powell, the BBC's controller of programmes. But by the time *A Year in Provence* was ready to run Jonathan had jumped ship to Carlton TV and the impetus slowed. We all worked so hard on it and we are all terribly sad that it didn't catch on with viewers. John Thaw should not carry the blame, although many viewers could not picture him as Peter Mayle when he was so entrenched in their minds as Inspector Morse. He did the best with what he had but there was no real plot. There was plenty to eat but no meat for him to get his acting teeth into.

'A large number of viewers found the language a problem. In the book most of the conversations Mayle had with the locals allowed them to talk to him in French. But the BBC took the decision not to have subtitles but to allow the French characters to speak in French, with John and Lindsay Duncan translating to each other as much as was necessary to inform the viewers of what was going on. But that just made for some laborious exchanges, especially for anyone who could speak a bit of French anyway.'

Even before *A Year in Provence* began filming Peter Mayle had expressed the hope that subtitles would not be used for the French characters. He said: 'There's nothing worse than getting the visuals right so the whole scene looks stunning and then getting a piece of dumb lettering going across the bottom of the screen so that no one looks at what they should.'

John Thaw remained philosophical about *A Year in Provence*. 'I had a disaster with that,' he admitted, 'but we're all allowed one. I was saddened because we all worked hard and hoped it would be enjoyed.'

He added: 'I won't accept it was bad. For God's sake, it was a half-hour of television once a week for twelve weeks. And from the reaction you'd think the BBC had decided to advocate the Euro-currency or something.' It did, however, persuade John that he should keep off television for a while. 'And I did think the next thing I do had better be good.' Happily for John, it was – *Kavanagh QC*.

10

KAVANAGH/RETURN
OF MORSE

John Thaw felt deeply injured by the *A Year in Provence* experience. What he had first imagined to be the ultimate dream job had turned into a public disaster, and a very rare embarrassment for an actor so used to his skills as a script-spotter and professional ability translating into ratings successes. As a result he was more than a little cautious when looking at the next project from the resourceful Ted Childs. The shrewd executive knew a slight change of gear was required for his most bankable star, so *Kavanagh QC* was born. James Kavanagh was devised by Childs as a crumpled yet charismatic northern barrister with an affection for the underdog. Kavanagh was born in Manchester, had a happy marriage that had just been tested by his feisty wife's recent waywardness, and a razor-sharp courtroom mind that could win over elderly judges even when they were awake. Who else but John Thaw could play the part? Yet he was not keen to recognize similarities with his own life.

At first he was reluctant. He did not want to wear a wig. He knew it sounded stupid, but John Thaw simply hates wearing hats and he did not want to spend months working underneath a hairy piece of history. Eventually he was persuaded that the headgear was now regarded as outdated by lawyers and was certain to have been discarded by the time filming began. The Bar Association was 99 per cent certain to dispense with the tradition. He cheerfully agreed to go ahead, only to find that the anti-wiggers were, surprisingly, outvoted.

'Ted Childs twisted my arm,' smiled John Thaw. 'By the time getting rid of the wigs did not happen I was hooked on Russell Lewis's script.' To help John feel that he didn't look 'a prat' he was advised to grow his hair longer so it curled down and showed underneath. In the family scenes, when Kavanagh was seen with his wife and children with his longer hair and jeans smart casual clothes, he certainly looked very different from the formal Inspector Morse.

The dialect was no problem, of course, because Kavanagh came from Thaw's home city. However, it was not quite as easy as you might think because, as he said: 'I couldn't just bring back my old accent. It would be too unbelievable because it was so thick. Kavanagh has lived in the south for twenty-five or thirty years so I decided just to flatten out the vowels because, unlike an actor, this guy doesn't have to lose an accent.

'James Kavanagh is a completely different character from Morse. He must be, otherwise I wouldn't have taken him on. For one thing he is a family man. He has climbed to the top of an elite profession to become one of the country's leading advocates, through sheer hard work and a love of the law. Kavanagh is a real challenge, as he is a working-class northerner operating in a upper-middle-class environment, working alongside all these toffee-nosed lawyers who went to Eton.' To research the role, Thaw visited London's Inns of Court and attended a murder trial at the Old Bailey. He said: 'Although the script is all there for you, I like to observe human behaviour and I ask a lot of questions. We also have a technical adviser in chambers who proved invaluable.'

Nevertheless, John found the countless courtroom scenes hard going: 'I understand why judges get crabby, stuck in those airless rooms, in one position, as it were. No wonder they adjourn cases at three in the afternoon. Unfortunately we couldn't do that. We were often stuck there until seven or eight at night.'

In real life John had been to court only once in his life, as the witness in a case about a man who left the scene of an accident, and it had not been an impressive experience. 'When I was giving evidence I was made to feel like I was the one on trial, that I was being prosecuted, because he had this sharp barrister,' said John. 'So I understand why people get terribly wary and nervous about being witnesses and things like that. Barristers can be frightening, especially in those silly wigs.'

The sight of John Thaw in a wig was anything but frightening to British television viewers. More than 12 million people voted with their remote controls to declare John's disastrous French leave had not affected his armchair audience appeal.

Kavanagh QC quickly joined the long list of successes, but the shy star refused to take all the credit. He said: 'The British love crime and anything to do with it. You could put on a series about judges' batmen and it would still get huge ratings. Maybe it is because we were lawless at one time and still are in our hearts. There's also an element of "there but for the grace of God go I" about these series, at least for me. You think, "Thank God that didn't happen to me." '

Long experience of life helped Thaw not to take himself too seriously. He knew his crusty court persona is part of the successful formula. When an observer commented that Kavanagh appeared happier in a later series John, quick as a flash, retorted: 'Does he? I'll have to put a stop to that.'

More seriously John said: 'One of the great virtues of *Kavanagh QC* is that the characters are believable. Barristers and solicitors say to me it is the nearest fictional portrayal so far to the real world of law. They say things like, 'I know people like him. I work with people like her.' On the whole they are pleased with what it does for the law. It tells it how it is and the problems they have. Not every case is cut and dried as sometimes it appears when you read the press report on it. You're not cheating the public, but at the same time you are hoping to make it interesting and entertaining, which after all is what it is all about.'

Sheila Hancock made a rare screen appearance alongside her husband in a memorable *Kavanagh* story, 'Blood Money', which was transmitted in March 1997. John was delighted when Sheila agreed to play the wife of a computer tycoon who died after an operation. He said: 'Obviously in the past I've read parts in scripts and thought, "Sheila could do this marvellously". But she is very choosy about what she does. I have never, much to my family's chagrin, put any of them up for parts. I never have done and I won't do. To be truthful it would be an extra burden on me, to be willing them to be good and worrying about them. Sheila and I have been on record years ago saying that we didn't want to work together too much because we didn't want to be 'the Lunts of Chiswick'. Although we met working together, we made a conscious decision that we would only do so if it happened that way.

' "Blood Money" was an example of that. As producer Chris Kelly said, "Sheila Hancock is a fine actress and I would like her in my show." It just so happens that I do his show.' Kavanagh represented Sheila's character in court and John said afterwards: 'Since I've been doing *Kavanagh QC*, I try not to share any problems I might have when I get home. It's a bit boring if you don't know what is going on. But since Sheila has filmed her episode she can now understand when I talk about, "Another bloody day in court today." '

Sheila first turned down the role and only changed her mind after talking to the production team and contributing her own thoughts on the character of Sarah Meadows, who was seeking to prosecute a doctor and a hospital trust. 'In the end it was a good part and that is what actors are always looking for,' she said. 'Casting directors often don't like casting married people together because it can bring a lot of extra resonances. Once John and I started filming "Blood Money", it was just like working with any good actor. We would often arrive at different times and go our separate ways when we had finished. Of course we had the odd gag but we didn't take our work home with us. John is not one to go over a scene with me.'

The two had last worked together ten years earlier, when Sheila appeared in an episode of the comedy *Home to Roost*.

The fourth series of *Kavanagh QC* was screened to high audiences and great critical acclaim in March and April 1998. John was particularly delighted when his old friend from RADA days, Tom Courtenay, guest-starred in the first episode, 'Memento Mori'. Written by Russell Lewis, it featured Courtenay as a mild-mannered doctor accused of killing his wife.

Thaw was over the moon when it was confirmed Tom Courtenay had accepted the part. 'I admire him so much as an actor and we hadn't worked together since the film which was a first for both Tom and me – *The Loneliness of the Long Distance Runner*.'

The story featured some highly charged courtroom clashes between Courtenay's character, Dr Felix Crawley, and Kavanagh. But although Courtenay relished the opportunity to revive his old friendship and wanted to work with Thaw, he admitted he still had to be pushed by his wife Isobel into accepting the role: 'I was being hesitant about taking on the part of a person I found very enigmatic. So finally she told me just to get on with it! Once I got used to the idea that he was a "nutcase", I was very happy with the role. There was plenty to go at.'

Tom remembered working with John before *The Loneliness of the Long Distance Runner*, on a black and white ITV drama called *The Lads*, set among a group of young soldiers on Cyprus. He said: 'Fairly soon after we shared the place in London it was obvious that John was going to be much more of a television actor than I was. I've no regrets about that and must admit I'm not much of a television watcher.'

Kavanagh's wife Lizzie, who had been played by Lisa Harrow, was somewhat abruptly killed off for the fourth series, which allowed the hero to get more involved in his work than before. Kavanagh was also shown doing his own cleaning. John said: 'That did provoke a lot of laughter among the crew. It may be the first time you've seen me on screen with a vacuum cleaner. But I do know how to plug it in and I am not unused to hoovering!'

The quality of the shows seemed better than ever and for John there was even a nostalgic trip back to his birth-place, which had strangely been rewritten as Bolton, for the filming of Rob Heyland's emotional story 'Care in the Community'. Kavanagh went north, with his attractive junior, Emma Taylor, played by Valerie Edmond, to defend a young man accused of murdering his baby daughter.

The filming took place in the Longsight area of Manchester where Thaw was born, and the actor noted: 'The house I grew up in had been pulled down, but we filmed in a high-rise block just ten minutes from there.'

Versatility had always been a feature of Thaw's appeal. Between *Kavanagh* series he appeared on television in a production of David Hare's *Absence of War*, in which he had already starred on stage at the National Theatre in 1993. He was widely praised for a performance which reminded critics that British television's greatest star knew how to dominate a theatre. His portrayal of principled but weak Labour leader George Jones was simply spell-bind-ing. Even if Neil Kinnock, who had given writer Hare remarkable access to life behind the scenes at the previous dismal election, was not exactly on his feet joining in the standing ovation.

Thaw brilliantly captured the dilemma of a political leader forced to compromise his deeply held beliefs with the realism born of the practical problems of getting elected. The actor believed Jones was a tragic hero. He said: 'He's a weak man in lots of ways, that's his problem. You are watching the tragedy of a man who can't get what he wants because of what he is. He is an honourable man and that gets in the way, because as he says in the play he cannot speak of what he believes.' John believed that was tragic on any level. 'And I don't think it is a situation confined to the Labour Party. I am sure it is true of many Tories and Liberals as well. Because they are all playing the game of politics and they want to win. I am sure John Major has many times made speeches and felt, "I'm not telling the truth. This is not what I really believe."'

John's typically forthright views on politics, expressed at the time, were very much in favour of more honesty. He wished it was somehow possible for politicians to be themselves and still survive in politics. 'I think the majority of the public would say the same. The public are not idiots. When they turn on the TV and see politicians ignoring questions and sliding out of answering them, they pick that up. I get annoyed. I get angry myself, as most people do, when I see a politician refusing to give a direct answer to a direct question. And they all do it.'

The inspiration for the story that brought *Morse* back to our screens in 1995 came from Colin Dexter's bird-watching son Jeremy. 'I got the idea for "The Way Through the Woods" after spending some time with Jeremy,' says Dexter. 'He is a very keen ornithologist, and my thoughts for the story started to gel when he was showing me three different sorts of woodpeckers.' It is partly based on the real-life murder of twenty-three-year-old Finnish student nurse Eila Karjalainen. Her remains were discovered in 1982, but the crime was never solved. The actors were offered a viewing of a police video construction of events but politely declined, as they preferred to concentrate on fiction in the script rather than the fact of a real tragedy.

It was three years since TV's most successful crime-fighting partnership of Inspector Morse and his faithful sidekick Lewis had last investigated foul deeds in the university city of Oxford. Even though John Thaw and Kevin Whateley had enjoyed world-wide success and critical acclaim for the first twenty-eight films featuring the thoughtful double act, both actors were apprehensive about the revival.

John Thaw's career had comfortably survived his French disappointments with the BBC's *A Year in Provence* and his portrayal of benevolent barrister Kavanagh QC had become yet another major ITV hit.

Kevin Whately's performances as popular Dr Jack Kerruish helped build up ratings success for *Peak Practice* and after leaving the medical drama he worked on the feature film *The English Patient* with Ralph Fiennes and Juliette Binoche, starred as a brutal husband in a harrowing BBC Screen One drama called *Trip Trap* and in his own series *The Broker's Man* as an accident-prone loss adjuster.

When they took a step back in time to reunite for 'The Way Through the Woods' both men had sleepless nights before filming started.

'It felt a bit like starting at a new school,' said John Thaw. 'When I did the very first scene of the film, a dinner date with Vivienne Ritchie's character, Claire Osborne, I was really very nervous. I thought, "Will Morse come back?"

'I had watched part of an episode the week before to remind myself of him, chiefly about Morse's tone of voice. I couldn't remember how he spoke!

'When we did the restaurant scene, I began to feel at home. I recognized a lot of the crew and of course I knew the director John Madden and producer Chris Burt. Within half an hour I felt as though I had never been away.'

Kevin said he felt exactly the same with his first scene. He was determined to make the new film live up to viewers' memories of the earlier heights. 'Morse and Lewis just seemed to click with the viewers,' said Kevin. 'And I always loved working with John. We stopped doing them before people got tired of them and I believe people are ready for another look at them now.'

Thaw explained: 'It was like getting on a bike again after it hadn't been ridden for years. Later that first day Kevin and I had our first scene together. Looking back I seem to recall it was in a pub, which seems appropriate!'

The relationship between the actors was still close, unaffected by Kevin's rise in status. John noted approvingly: 'We always shared a caravan on *Morse* right from the beginning and this time was no exception. In fact, I believe Kevin asked for that. They assumed at first that now he was a "star" he would want his own.'

While the two friends were delighted to be in harness together again on screen the writers sparked up the conflict between Morse and Lewis, as the dogged chief inspector re-examined an old case much against his faithful assistant's better judgement. With Lewis pushing for his long-delayed promotion the young man lost his temper for once with Morse and called him 'a miserable, self-centred, arrogant bastard'. *Inspector Morse* was certainly back with a bang.

Even though the return was a smash hit, John remained cautious about committing himself far into the future. 'I'm getting past retirement age as a copper,' he insisted. 'There's a detective on German TV called Inspector Derrick and the same actor has been playing the part for something like twenty-seven years. He must be in his seventies and he is always filmed sitting behind a desk or in a car. He's too old to move about much. I don't want to be like that – here comes Inspector Morse and his Zimmer frame.'

John Thaw's popularity with the audience was certainly still there. The return of Inspector Morse in 'The Way Through the Woods' was watched by 16.56 million people, an amazing 65 per cent of the TV audience. The next year he did almost as well with 'The Daughters of Cain' and the cerebral detective was revived as a much loved annual event.

In November 1997 the memorable 'Death is Now My Neighbour' featured John Thaw's old neighbour Richard Briers threatening to steal the show, with a wonderful portrayal of malicious retiring college master Sir Clixby Bream. But Morse, with his first name now publicly exposed as Endeavour, had a trick left up his sleeve. He delighted millions of faithful fans of the show by at long last embarking on a love affair with the beautiful and brilliant music teacher Adele Cecil, played by Judy Loe.

Happily, the fragrant Adele appeared again in the final Inspector Morse story, *The Wench is Dead*, screened in autumn 1998. Morse is in hospital after he collapses during an Oxford academic conference on Victorian crime. While recovering in the Radcliffe Infirmary, he is visited by Adele and American scholar Millie Van Buren, whose book on the Oxford canal murder in the summer of 1859 begins to obsess a Morse increasingly irritated by his incarceration. Morse becomes more and more convinced that the two boatmen who were hanged for the murder of the respectable Mrs Joanna Franks were victims of a gross miscarriage of justice.

For the first time he does not have Sergeant Lewis to bully and browbeat. The programme-makers were unable to persuade Kevin Whately to play the role, in spite of an offer of more than £175,000 for some three weeks' work. So young graduate police constable Adrian Kershaw, played by twenty-four-year-old newcomer Matthew Finney, is co-opted by Morse to help in the historic investigation. Sadly the film ends with Morse's retirement from the force. This time it looked as though it really might be the end for Inspector Morse.

11

SHEILA

In 1988 television's happiest marriage broke up in a flurry of large and unpleasant headlines. Sheila moved out of the family home and show business sadly shook its head. If rich and successful John Thaw and Sheila Hancock, who had always appeared so happy and ideally suited to each other, could not make it, then who could?

Sheila tried to explain afterwards. 'It wasn't so much that there was something wrong with our marriage, as something wrong with me. I had gutbusted my way through life then suddenly I found myself stuck in a terrible rut. I hadn't been thinking about where I was going or what I was doing. I was living my life entirely by habit and everything seemed completely out of control. My marriage was going up the spout and there was absolutely nothing I could do about it. So I rented a tiny little house with next to no furniture, and lived virtually out of a suitcase. It was like going back to how I'd begun. I didn't want my possessions, only to live as simply as possible.

'I did very little work and just spent my time listening to music, walking and meeting friends, most of whom thought I'd gone mad. But I wanted to shed my responsibilities, and to get away before something terrible happened. Of course I worried how John would deal with the situation, but I knew that my not being there was better than what had been happening previously. And I knew that neither of us could take much more. Leaving home wasn't a courageous move for me – there was nothing brave about it – there was simply no other choice.'

Their daughters were deeply concerned. Elly Jane felt that it was not a separation in the true sense, more of a breathing space that arrived to relieve a particularly difficult and stressful time. She knew many factors had combined with Sheila's illness to create this situation and in fact the family continued to see a lot of each other throughout the marital hiccough. Both she and Abigail agreed that once their parents had gone through their crisis they'd come back together even stronger than before. They all rallied round to help and they were all delighted that the marriage survived.

In September Sheila left for a three-month tour of the Middle East that some friends thought spelled the end of the marriage. Yet she was back for Christmas and the warmth of the family celebrations helped to rekindle John and Sheila's love.

The couple gradually came back together again. John certainly believed it was a painful separation but one which refreshed the marriage: 'It was not the sort of separation where one said, "We must separate. Then we'll come back and it will be better." It was not done in that sort of cold way. Sheila had been ill and just wanted and needed to be on her own. It was a question of "when" we get back together, it was not a question of "if". Sheila just needed that space and that time to adjust after being told she had cancer.

'I was doing *Morse* at that time, working long irregular

hours and then still having a certain amount of work to do when I got home. Of course I was not as supportive as I would like to have been. So, therefore, for Sheila the only answer was to be on her own.'

John clearly felt that the time apart was one of those unfortunate phases that can strike any marriage or relationship. They were working very hard and therefore not together nearly as much as they might have been and the pressures and strains built up until Sheila did something about it. John always knew that Sheila was his best friend, the first person he would go to if he was in trouble or unhappy. He was close to being a workaholic and a man who found it very difficult to relax. His concentration on a part was total as he always insisted on giving 100 per cent effort to any role he undertook. That took its toll on him and sometimes on those closest to him.

He now tried to say 'No' more often, but in his heart he knew he still worked too hard. And even when he was not working he was never able to switch off from acting completely. Even when he was not actually making a series he was frequently mentally rehearsing the next one. That was what he called being relaxed! He might go shopping or go for a walk or do some cooking. He might listen to music or go to the theatre, but always somewhere in the back of his mind John found there was a niggling little thought that there was a job coming up soon.

He puts down at least part of his difficulties in dealing with women to his all-male background. There was no woman around the house while he was growing up so he never observed any guidelines about how women behaved. He was terribly shy and frequently ended up putting women on a pedestal. At school John was totally besotted by the beautiful young Asian girl Alison Lui. In his first marriage he fell head over heels with Sally Alexander yet failed fully to understand her frustrations at being left at home with a young baby while he was out being a television star. It took him most of a lifetime to begin to find out how women tick. Gradually, with time, after a quarter of a century with Sheila and their daughters, more understanding developed.

'The honest truth is that I prefer women to men,' he said. 'I live in a household of women which I enjoy enormously and I simply feel happier in women's company. I have men friends of course, and I exclude them from this, but I find men tend to be competitive and try to impress all the time. With women there is no threat. I can just talk to them like an ordinary person. They don't want to impress. They don't want to compete. They don't want to tell you the story of their lives, like a lot of men do for some reason I have never been able to fathom. Some men think you're bound to be fascinated in the details of what they did last week, or what they did a year ago. So I much prefer the company of women.

'I don't think of myself as a man's man. Obviously I have male friends like Dennis Waterman and Kevin Whately, whom I get on with very well. But the other male friends I have are mainly workmates – my stand-in, the wardrobe master, the bloke who does my make-up. I enjoy their company and I have them on almost everything I do. But I'm always more relaxed with women than I am with men. Women are not so combative. They just take people at face value, whereas a lot of men see things with an ulterior motive, they're trying to impress you, or antagonize you. I don't like going to pubs – that sort of social occasion I find boring. Who can be the funniest, who can be the toughest, all that.'

After the split was healed Sheila observed with typically brutal frankness: 'If John went off with a sixteen-year-old nubile blonde I would absolutely loathe it, but it would not be the end of my life. I would survive. I have lived apart from him before and, although I would hate to have to do it again, I could if I had to. I don't like being on top of anybody all the time anyway, I like being on my own sometimes, I really do. And so does John, hugely. Those spaces are very valuable.'

John said: 'Her health is fine now and as far as we are concerned she is fine. Cured.' The real impact of Sheila's health scare was colossal on her husband. He used all of his acting skills to disguise just how concerned he was about the awful possibility of losing his wife. One of the decisions he took was to curtail his drinking. He might not really be a whisky-swilling soak like Jack Regan or a real-ale bore like Inspector Morse, but John Thaw always enjoyed a drink. He said: 'At various times in my life I've been a drinker, there is no question about that. But I hasten to add that it has never affected my work.' John's strong work ethic always made him frown on anyone who drinks on the job. Actors with a drink problem never seemed to last long on any Thaw production. He set very high standards and woe betide anyone who failed to measure up.

'I never drank while I was working, although afterwards, particularly when I was doing *The Sweeney* with Dennis Waterman, I would go into the pub and have a few drinks. But I'm getting too old for it now. I would wake up in the morning feeling bad. When you are younger you can shrug it off. A lot of my friends have given it up. I read about Anthony Hopkins giving up and saying he had never felt better in his life. All these guys, and Peter O'Toole was another, have given it up. They were all preaching that it was so good and that you felt better, so I thought I would give it a go myself to see what it was like. I found it was so easy to do, like giving up sugar in tea. I remember giving up sugar years ago, and although at first I thought I would never manage it, from that day to this I have never had any sugar in tea or coffee.'

Sheila prefers not to discuss the cancer too much in public because she rightly believes that it might make people think she is still ill, which could affect her chances of getting work. She became a vegetarian on the advice of the Bristol Cancer Help Centre and her husband was deeply sympathetic to her need for a change of diet.

Sheila said: 'I think my illness came as a shock not only to me but also to John and the children. It brings you up against the possibility of great change and now great change doesn't have any large fears for me. I suppose that is what I mean about John going. I would simply loathe it but now I know I have the ability to make changes to adjust to make the best of me.

'People think that John and I are completely different characters but we are much more alike than they know. We laugh at exactly the same things. And the longer you are together with someone the more you find it is wonderful to be so relaxed with them. John and I were talking the other day about when, years ago, one of the girls was going through a bit of a torment about the fellows. He said, "Thank God that's over," and I said, "Yes." I genuinely felt that.

'You move into a purer kind of love where it's not all game-playing and "Will he phone or won't he phone?" All that wondering, "Have I said the right thing?" is over. I just say the first thing that comes into my head and it doesn't matter.

'John and I have similar taste in music as well. He is more knowledgeable about it than I am, and that is wonderful because he often introduces me to things that he has heard and I haven't. We're not avid theatregoers. So often we have gone and wanted to leave in the first interval and haven't been able to because we know people in the cast.

'John is not very sociable. It is an awful effort for him because he is terribly shy. He is all right with a film crew when he knows everyone, but take him out to a dinner party and he sits there with a miserable expression on his face all night. He hates it. The experience is agony for him. Unless it is people he knows really, really well and then he is OK. But really he just isn't interested and we have so little time together that often we don't want other people around.'

When John was in residence at their Chiswick home they hardly ever entertained. Richard Briers and his wife or other old friends used to come round occasionally. And until his sad death in 1997 John's father was a regular visitor, with his wife Mildred.

'Anybody else who comes into our house is amazingly privileged,' said Sheila. 'Because John hates people coming in. When he was away when the girls were still at home we used to entertain all right. We'd go mad and have masses of people in.'

John's reputation as a sex symbol became something of a family joke, especially when women readers of the raunchy magazine *Forum* voted him one of the world's sexiest men, but Sheila admits there was a time when she did not find it quite so funny. 'I think it bothered me when I was younger,' she said. 'If ever he chooses to leave home then that's it but I am pretty certain he won't. He's funny, he's a real home body. And he has never, ever been a womanizer.'

John's first wife and Sheila are now firm friends and they agree that he was a very loyal man. 'Loyalty is a strong trait in him,' said Sheila. 'He is loyal to Ted Childs, the man from Central Television behind *Inspector Morse*, and to companies he works for, as well as to me and the family.

'Mind you, I'm always saying to him, "You're far too old for me," because sometimes he can be very boring. He won't go out, he just wants to stay in and put his feet up and watch the telly.

'I know acting couples where there is rivalry but not with us. Even if I did used to get a bit miffed when I was only doing the odd radio play while John was off every day to be Inspector Morse. But then I am better at being out of work than John is, because I have a lot of other things that I do. He hates it. He is awful when he is out of work.'

Sheila openly admires the gritty determination with which John approached his work: 'My husband, coming from a similar background to me, is propelled by the attitude of "I'll show the bastards". Mine, despite my father's competitive spirit, is "I probably won't".

'I am very fond of *Inspector Morse*. I think John makes a marvellous job of it. But then he is good at whatever he does. He has this extraordinary ability to get right inside a part. He isn't really like Morse, but he is a lot nearer than he was to Jack Regan.'

Sheila and John were not enchanted when daughter Joanna expressed a desire to become wealthy. Sheila said: 'Money was never a motivation for me and nor was it for John. Certainly when Joanna was finishing school one of the things on the list of what she wanted was a lot of money.

'It amazed us. We are lucky that we are very comfortable. Equally I don't think either of us would care very much if we lost it all. With our backgrounds we know life can be OK without a lot of money. I enjoy the success but I think eventually we will move to a much smaller house. We are very happy together, very happy indeed. But I think that one of the ways I have matured is that I don't need other people so much as I used to.

'I have been on my own and I quite like being on my own. I would hate to be without John but, unlike some women, my life would not end my if husband and I parted. And the same goes for John. We have other things in our lives than one another, but having him is jolly nice, jolly nice indeed. A great bonus.'

In the garden of the old Chiswick home, which slopes down to the river where you can stand under apple trees and watch the boats go by, there is a grotto hidden under some branches. In the mosaic alcove are embedded the words: 'The best in this kind are but shadows.' John said: 'Sheila had that made. It's about actors. It's there to remind us that, however good you may have been on the night, it's finished. It puts it all into perspective.'

Once youngest daughter Joanna had left home the Thaws could see no reason to keep their sprawling Chiswick family home. They moved their main home to a stylish country house near Malmesbury in Wiltshire, keeping a small base in the capital for convenience and their home in Provence for get away-from-it-all holidays. Sheila said: 'We moved to the country because the children have grown up and the house is miles too big for us. It's ridiculous for just the two of us to rattle round in.'

John said: 'We were often saying how nice to be in the

country so one day we said, "Well, bugger this, why don't we do the opposite of what most people do? Make London our weekend place and our main house in the country?" And that's what we did. Sheila is like me, we both want more time at home. We've both been rushing around doing things.'

When they were first married John admitted he was not always the easiest man to live with. There were black moods. He was sometimes reticent and uncommunicative but Sheila helped him to overcome all that. 'I'm far less intense now and that's due to Sheila's help. It's been trial and error on her part. There's been no magic formula. She's helped me learn to talk through my problems. Early in our relationship I didn't talk enough. I wouldn't share my worries because I thought I should solve them on my own. But life is not like that. I was brought up believing that boys shouldn't cry. I suppose I thought it was unmasculine to admit failures. But now we all have problems, failures. Now I share mine with Sheila. And often bore the pants off her. At the risk of sounding rather ancient, the older I get the more important home becomes. Everyone needs a base and roots. And we all need love. Sadly some people, like Morse, haven't got it. I just thank God that I have.'

The need for love goes right back to his earliest days. As a seven-year-old boy, John cried and cried when his mother walked out on the family. The feeling of rejection was almost unbearable at times. As they grew up, the young brothers could never quite comprehend how their mother could leave them behind when the marriage broke up. It was an appalling experience that haunted him all his life. John became a great believer in the institution of marriage and a fierce opponent of infidelity. He loathed the whole idea of illicit affairs and saw loyalty as one of the most important facets of personality.

He also had a remarkable determination which drove his career forever onwards and upwards. He had vivid childhood memories of the tallyman coming every Friday with the payments book, after his father had been forced to borrow money to buy clothes. He was always resolute that he would never go back to that again. John's initial inferiority complex, which caused him some terrible traumas during his early difficult months at RADA, long since subsided. He was wise enough and rich enough to enjoy life to the full.

He would much rather discuss his love for cars, for instance, than his innermost emotions. John Thaw was a very fast driver. He loved convertibles and sometimes drove a Saab Turbo with an open top and gave his beloved old MGB to Sheila. 'I drove the MGB for twelve years and then I had it restored and refurbished by the man who does such a good job on Morse's old Jaguar. It's twenty-two years old now and I love it. MGBs are beautiful cars. I changed the colour, which real enthusiasts say you should never do, from the original harvest gold to a lovely creamy white.

'Sheila was delighted to get the car as a present. She drives it in the summer and carefully puts it in the garage for the winter. Being a typical woman it wasn't enough just throwing her the keys and saying, "Here you are darling, that's yours now." I had to write to Swansea and get the registration document changed into her name. Just so she was sure that it was actually hers. I love that car. I look after it myself. Well, I know where the oil goes and things like that. We also used to have an old Rover V8. It was very stylish at the time. My daughters remember how we were always having to pull off the motorway for one of them to be sick because it was so smooth a drive.

'I've always liked cars. My very first car was the Triumph Vitesse I bought from my first father-in-law. It was wonderful and went very fast. Then I had a Ford Cortina GT and later an MG. After that I got my first MGB, my first roadster, a lovely blue one that I eventually sold to Dennis Waterman because he nagged me so much.

'Touch wood I've only had one thing on my licence. It was 1967 and I was filming and we had an electrician strapped on the bonnet, filming me driving. Nobody had checked that the road was clear, there was a parked car and we went into the back of it. Luckily there was nobody in it. On the whole the police are very favourable but right from *The Sweeney* days there's always been one element of the police who intensely dislike me, or other people who play policemen. They see what they think are poofy actors mincing about pretending to be tough coppers and that gets up their nose.

'I used to long for the sun to come out so I could put the top down on the Saab. I love driving down to our place in Provence with the weather gradually improving all the way. I like the feeling of power in a car but I don't drive particularly fast,' he says, then the face crumples into the familiar grin and he admits: 'Well, actually I do. I like the fact that the power is there if I need it. The Saab was my first automatic car. I got it because I was sick of going through London forever changing gear. The traffic just seems to get worse.'

Yet John Thaw was horrified at the idea of the ultimate motor, a Rolls-Royce. Although he could afford his own fleet of the world's most expensive cars the actor cringed at the idea of flaunting affluence so openly.

'They are much too ostentatious,' he said. 'People stare at you.' Thaw's first wife had a Rolls-Royce-driving father and he confided to his son-in-law that he felt it had arrived too late. 'He said he was past the age when he could really enjoy the car,' John recalled years later. 'And that he wished he had had the courage to buy one when he was a young man instead of struggling to buy a house. He reckoned he would have appreciated it more.

'But I don't agree. I have friends who have Rollers and I don't even like to be near them. I borrowed one once when I dropped a pal of mine at the airport and he said I could use it while he was away. But I didn't want to drive around in it. People stare at you and sneer.'

Later John drove the new Jaguar Sovereign XJ8 while Sheila has an XK8 from the same stable. John borrowed the sports model from Jaguar and Sheila fell in love with the elegant motor. He bought it for her as an early twenty-fifth wedding anniversary present.

John said: 'When I was a kid I wanted a Jag. Some kids wanted a Rolls-Royce but I thought the Jag was gorgeous. Now, because Morse's car is so popular, I often get people asking "Where's the real Jag?"'

12

NEW HEROES

John Thaw finished work on the fourth series of *Kavanagh QC* in the autumn of 1997 knowing that his next role – and his appearance – were to be radically different. He was to play the outwardly curmudgeonly and white-bearded widower, Tom Oakley, in a wartime drama called *Goodnight Mister Tom*; a two-hour film adaptation of the bestselling book by Michelle Magorian.

John had jumped at the chance to star in 'a real family film', as he put it. The moving story about a bond that grows between an old man and a nine-year-old evacuee foisted upon him from London appealed enormously to John from the outset.

The poignant story starts in Tom Oakley's village of Little Weirwold on the day war is declared in 1939. Part of a crocodile of children from London's East End, Willie Beech is billeted on Tom in his cottage overlooking the church and the graveyard where Tom's wife and son lie buried. The placement is in accordance with Mrs Beech's written instructions that Willie is housed with someone who is either religious or lives near a church.

Before long Tom realizes that Willie continually expects the worst because of the deprivations he has had to endure in London at the hands of his strict mother. Her introductory letter warning that Willie is 'full of sin' is accompanied by an ugly, thick leather belt. The sight of this or Tom's fireside poker strikes a patent fear into the boy.

But gradually a friendship grows between the unlikely partners as Tom takes on the job of improving Willie's reading and writing abilities and fosters his natural talent for drawing. Willie's anxieties are smoothed away and life in Little Weirwold becomes an idyll of fishing trips with Tom and the village children, locals and evacuees, and the home comforts of Tom's cottage. But just as Willie celebrates his tenth birthday surrounded by his new friends, his mother summons him back to the unexpected terrors of Blitz-torn London.

After filming a new series of *Kavanagh* and another *Inspector Morse, Goodnight Mister Tom* presented John with a refreshing new challenge in the spring of 1998. 'It has something for everyone,' he said of the story, 'because in a way it's about everyone. We've all been children. We've all felt frightened, we've all felt unloved, and loved, hopefully.'

For the character of Tom Oakley and the feel of the period John was able to draw on the real stories of wartime evacuation from *Mister Tom*'s director Jack Gold and, closer to home, from his wife Sheila Hancock. Both had experienced the upheaval of evacuation, just two children among millions of people who were moved from areas considered likely targets for the bombs of the German Luftwaffe.

'Sheila was evacuated from the centre of London twice during the war – and hated it,' John explained. 'We spoke about this and she had also made a film for the BBC about the experience so during filming I'd ask her the odd question about it all. Jack Gold had also been evacuated for a short while, although I think he had a better time.

'When some of these children were evacuated, you had problems of the different cultures: city kids going to a country place where the locals would never have met anyone from London. So you got the country kids, quite naturally, feeling their territory was invaded by these city kids and it must have been hard for friendships to grow in that situation.'

As he frequently does when he is not working, John grew a beard and with half a mind on *Mister Tom* he decided he would simply let it grow and see how it turned out. 'I often have a beard partly out of laziness because it saves me ten or fifteen minutes a day shaving,' said John as his white whiskers began to sprout profusely. 'I was always aware that the director or the producer might say, "We hate that, get it off, you'll frighten the children," but they liked it. You could say it made me look like a benign Santa Claus, or a sane King Lear. But in the book Tom grows a beard halfway through so I thought I'd go the whole hog and have one. It added another physical dimension to being different.

'The character of Tom Oakley was very different from the other two roles I'd played that year, Morse and Kavanagh. You could say they are well-educated, sophisticated, urbane people whereas Mister Tom is the opposite of that, probably not well-educated, taught in a village school, and certainly not urbane.

'He's just a natural man with instincts as opposed to intellect. His instinct on this occasion is his love for Willie Beech. He empathizes with this little lad and what he's gone through. He knows, as an animal knows, what this child needs and gives it to him and Willie, thank God, responds in almost an animal-like way to Tom's affection and protection.'

Although he had worked on an episode of *Black Beauty* many years before, it had been a long time since John had worked with children so he thought it would be prudent to meet up with twelve-year-old Nick Robinson, who was to play Willie, before they started filming together. They met up at casting director Joyce Nettles's home and the young lad's reaction was one of awe. 'I said to myself, "I can't believe he's here, in real life,"' Nick recalls of that first sighting of John.

Young Nick might have been just twelve years old but he was already something of a stage veteran. He had appeared in the National Theatre production of *An Inspector Calls* at the Aldwych Theatre in London's West End and with Juliet Stevenson in *The Chalk Circle*. When he landed the role of Willie in *Goodnight Mister Tom* he was appearing with the Royal Shakespeare Company in Ibsen's *Little Eyolf* at the Barbican.

Any qualms John may have had about forging a good working relationship with Nick were instantly dispelled. It was a harmonious acting partnership and John was full of admiration for the youngster. 'He has tremendous stamina,' John remarked at the end of a long day. 'He worked in scenes that took a few hours and he'd be as on the ball at the end as he was at the beginning.'

Mister Tom was shot in April and May of 1998 and the weather was the worst John could ever remember encountering in all his years of filming. 'It rained every day,' he recalls, 'and if there was one show where the last thing you wanted was rain, it was this one. But the camera team did a wonderful job in making the countryside look far better than it was in reality.'

Despite the elements, John's thoughtful performance and a screenplay by Brian Finch that added an adult perspective to what is essentially a children's book, earned *Goodnight Mister Tom* some excellent reviews.

In October of 1998 John's remarkable career was recognized by the television industry when he was given the Lifetime Achievement Award in the prestigious National Television Awards. A packed celebrity audience at the Royal Albert Hall gave him a huge ovation when he went up to collect his trophy. With wife Sheila proudly looking on, John dedicated the award to her and their upcoming twenty-fifth wedding anniversary.

Just a few weeks later John was back on screen making his thirty-second appearance as the Oxford detective in *The Wench is Dead*, the new two-hour film of *Inspector Morse*. The film attracted its usual huge audience and there was further encouraging news for Morse's followers.

'While we were making *The Wench is Dead*, it was thought likely to be the last one,' said John. 'Colin Dexter had stopped writing and there wasn't another book to adapt. But in the meantime I've been told he was writing another book so we'll have to see if we can get another good script out of it. And then we'd have to see if I was free to do it. In the end, we'd all have to be in agreement about doing a new Morse.

'I don't know whether, if Kevin Whately was asked to do another one, he would want to wipe the slate clean and start again. It's up to him obviously. He might say: "Yes, great, when do we start?" I certainly wouldn't say, I won't do another one because Kevin's not in it. It would just have to be extra good to be worth doing without him.'

ITV and John Thaw agreed that five series of the benevolent barrister were enough and, after he bowed out with an excellent final series in early 1999, John spent the rest of the year taking up new challenges. Perhaps the biggest surprise to his army of armchair followers was to see John Thaw playing a doctor for the first time in the two-part ITV drama *Plastic Man*. And they were even more surprised to see him locked in a torrid affair. John thoroughly enjoyed himself moving into new areas as ace plastic surgeon Joe MacConnell.

He said, 'I am squeamish about anything bloody. This is the first time I have played a medical man. I would never watch one of those documentaries about heart surgery, so I was pleased to know *Plastic Man* was not to be ITV's answer to *Casualty*. I would never have had the stomach to be a real life surgeon.

'We were filming at Hillingdon Hospital and there were all these medical magazines in the set of my character's office. One was called *The Plastic Surgeon*, it was probably very appealing to a plastic surgeon but to the layman it was very gory. That was halfway through the afternoon. I was very glad I didn't happen to see it first thing in the morning. But Joe MacConnell is mainly involved in restorative surgery; helping people coping with breast cancer or the results of road accidents or birthmarks. I find it fascinating what they can do, because they can change people's lives just by removing a disfigurement like a birthmark. The only research I did was from the script. I read it and then talked to our advisor, who was a top plastic surgeon. I bored him to death with questions, but he was on hand to help us get it right.'

The enormous appeal of *Plastic Man* was that it took John Thaw into areas beyond the professional for once. MacConnell was a happily married man, a pillar of the community, who fell in love with a beautiful colleague, played by Frances Barber, a fully paid-up member of the Inspector Morse Drama Society. 'The strength of *Plastic Man* is that it explores Joe MacConnell's emotional problems as well as the medical situations he deals with. It is very rich in that sense. In *Morse*, for example, you never ventured into his family at all. This character has far more depth than I have been allowed to show in either *Morse* or *Kavanagh QC*. Joe MacConnell is a much more rounded character.'

John clearly revelled in the role: 'Morse was totally enigmatic, but MacConnell is very open about his emotions and feelings. Again, that is why this role is different from anything I have done before. Within Joe MacConnell you can see both sides of a person. One is the professional, the other a human being who most people will relate better to than they related to Morse. They admired Morse and liked to watch him, but he was never the guy next door. With MacConnell, you imagine you could sit down and have a drink with him and talk to him about your problems.'

More than twelve million viewers did just that as John Thaw's massive pulling power worked again with the fascinating tale. And John's performance as Joe wrestling with his love for his wife played by Sorcha Cusack and his passion for the clinical psychologist played by Frances Barber. Many fans were shocked when the overwhelmingly decent Joe took the plunge and embarked on his affair. John thoroughly enjoyed the emotional demands of the role.

'Over the years, I have struggled to make myself come out of the character and it often depends on what you have been doing during the day's filming. If you've been drinking coffee in the scene and talking about football, it's not a problem.

'But I do get a hangover from a scene that involves mental anguish. You just learn to step out of the role and go forward to whatever you're doing that night in your own life. Without sounding like a selfish luvvie, it's your instinct to stay with the role until the next day. MacConnell has been married for thirty years or so and he has three children. His daughter is an anaesthetist at the same hospital and his eldest son is at medical school. The younger boy is still at school. I can relate to that because it's a similar pattern to myself. I have three daughters, two of whom are both acting and the third is doing a post graduate course at LAMDA. Melanie has done *A Touch of Frost* and Abigail was in *Vanity Fair*. Joanna is the one still studying, so she looks after the kids when the others are rehearsing. We have three grandchildren under the age of three,' he added proudly.

John felt the strong script came along at the right time in his life. 'You have to be my age and have been through marriage, relationships and children. The part relies on having been a parent and reaching a certain age. I should stress that I have never personally had an affair, but I can imagine the devastation it would cause. It was not hard for me to do that.'

And John Thaw had more new developments to come. His next television project was to be playing the title role in a major new ITV series called *Renard*. John says, 'He is a priest in a small town in Nazi-occupied France in the Second World War. It starts with the German invasion in 1940 and follows this remarkable man. It is very adventurous. And I am also filming *The Waiting Time*, a post-Cold War thriller in which I play a solicitor's clerk.'

John Thaw insisted that working hard kept him fit. 'I don't envisage ever giving it up, unless it gives me up. I don't really want to do long series or theatre now, but I will take on the parts that are worth getting out of bed for.'

13

THE REMORSEFUL DAY

On 16 September 1999, sightseers in London's Piccadilly Circus were stopped in their tracks by the following news flashed up in lights on a giant screen:

INSPECTOR MORSE 1930–1999, RIP

It was electrifying news in every sense.

The dramatic announcement of Morse's death up in lights was, in fact, an artfully conceived way of launching his creator Colin Dexter's final Morse mystery, *The Remorseful Day*, in which the chief inspector was to be finally killed off by a heart attack. As the novel hit the bookstalls that day, it immediately became clear that Dexter had indeed passed the death sentence on his detective chief inspector after 32 TV films and 13 novels spanning 25 years.

By Dexter's side, as the death knell sounded for Morse in Piccadilly, was John Thaw himself, anxious after the bad news to pass on the good news that he would play Chief Inspector Morse one last time in a TV version of *The Remorseful Day*. 'When Colin was writing it, I said I'd do it on the basis that it really was the last one,' said John. 'Colin assured me it was. I didn't want it to be like Frank Sinatra's endless farewell concerts. That said, it's a great pity the old chap's got to go because people will miss him and I will be as sad as a lot of viewers.'

Colin Dexter explained that he had plotted Morse's death because he wanted to give up the 'lonely, demanding discipline of writing'.

He said: 'Morse has lived with me for more than a quarter of a century and I shall miss him. His health has been steadily poorer over the past few years, and his excessive consumption of alcohol has probably been the main cause. With the body count now risen to almost eighty, Oxford has become the murder capital of the UK, and the time has come to put an end to this.'

Morse's final moments were filmed at St Peter's Hospital, Chertsey, three days before the end of shooting. 'I woke up on the day of filming itself thinking, Bloody hell, this is it!' remembers Kevin Whately, who had jumped at the chance to return in his role of Lewis one last time. 'We were quite busy with all the other scenes, but obviously Morse's death lurked in the back of everyone's minds.'

The actual shooting of Morse's demise proved to be a somewhat spooky business. 'We filmed it with a hand-held camera,' John recalled, 'and the odd thing was that the camera wouldn't work. It was really strange. The producer thought there was some spiritual element about that. Everything was checked three times and still the camera wouldn't function. In the end we took a ten-minute break and eventually the camera did work and we filmed it in one take.'

By the time *The Remorseful Day* was due to be screened, on 15 November 2000, Morse was destined to undergo the most public and predictable demise ever seen on British television. The final film was awaited with a mixture of fascination and sorrow.

In the event, nearly 14 million viewers tuned in to watch the episode – a twisting story in which the body count rose to four before Morse breathed his last in a hospital bed. He had been rushed into intensive care after collapsing, eyes bulging, clutching his chest, on to the grass in Exeter College quad. In the background could be heard the strains of Fauré's Requiem Mass from a college choir rehearsal. A passing don, mistaking the stricken Morse for a drunk, remarked distastefully to his companion: 'A bit early in the day!'

But Colin Dexter did not allow Morse's days to end on such a sour note. He allowed him to die with dignity. Morse's final words on his deathbed were: 'Thank Lewis for me.' The absent Lewis had already been dispatched by Morse to Heathrow Airport to stop the prime suspect in their final murder case from boarding a plane.

The ultimate, poignant words were left to Lewis as he returned to pay his last respects in the mortuary. Uncovering Morse's head, he planted a kiss on his forehead. 'Goodbye, sir,' he said softly.

At 10.30 on the night of 15 November, Chief Inspector Morse passed on into the TV archives and next morning the *Daily Express* summed up the general feeling by declaring: 'The nation was in mourning last night after the death of its most celebrated sleuth. Inspector Endeavour Morse suffered a heart attack brought on by diabetes. He was 70.'

John Thaw's last performance as Morse was widely praised. 'It was a beautifully done death,' said *The Times*, and the *Sunday Times* commented:

> His dying moments included many of the elements that have made Morse so popular over the years: the pleasant scenery, the background music, and a fine

performance from John Thaw. Even in mid-heart attack, he managed to make Morse look annoyed at the interruption of his investigation. If the inspector had lived, he would have charged his heart with wasting police time.

For John Thaw, Morse's death was something of a release. 'All good things come to an end,' he said. 'When I saw him dead I had a mental flashback of the fifteen years I've been playing him – all the stories, all the various locations, all the different actors and actresses, and it all ends with a human being in a morgue.

'In a way it was a good thing that he died rather than driving off into the Oxford sunset. That was much better than if he had retired to live in Lyme Regis. In a couple of years ITV would have asked me to do one more, set in Lyme Regis, and the trouble is I probably would have been tempted. But this way it's out of my hands. Morse as a character doesn't exist any more. That means that his death was good for me professionally.

It's fair to say that *Inspector Morse* changed the landscape of British TV. Two-hour police dramas were nonexistent before *Inspector Morse*. The global impact was no less powerful: the series attracted around 750 million viewers in 40 countries, and 1 billion people in 200 countries around the world were reckoned to have seen at least one episode, including 85 per cent of the British population.

By one of the quirks prone to his profession, John soon found himself back at St Peter's Hospital, Chertsey, the very same hospital where Morse had breathed his last. This time he was there to film a scene for a new series of *Kavanagh QC* in which James visited Samantha Bond's character Sarah. 'I have to say, it was strange to find myself fit and well and back where I'd "died" earlier in the year, especially after all the attention that Morse's death received!' John remarked.

The cast and crew also went back to Oxford for further *Kavanagh QC* scenes shot in the city's town hall, playing London's Royal Courts of Justice. Many who spotted John out and about in Oxford were thoroughly confused and wondered if Morse was to make a miraculous comeback and rise from the dead.

But later it was indeed the Morse connection that took John, his wife Sheila and Kevin Whately to the same town hall to see Colin Dexter being given the Freedom of his adopted city. John was delighted to join Colin and his wife Dorothy for the occasion, although he and Kevin seemed to spend most of their time at the reception signing autographs for councillors and other guests.

With Morse having gone to meet his maker and John preparing to hang up his wig and gown as *Kavanagh QC* drew to a close after a hugely successful run, there was a hunger shared by John and his close working associates to find a new drama series for the actor. It soon presented itself in *Monsignor Renard*, an ambitious new series from the writer Russell Lewis with John in the title role as a French Roman Catholic priest returning from Spain to his small home town in northern France during the early stages of World War Two.

The programme had great potential, depicting the traumas Renard and the townsfolk faced as they lived side by side with the occupying German army. It would explore Renard's efforts to help his flock during eight dangerous months in 1940.

One of the reasons John was attracted to the role of Renard was the appeal of playing a priest for the first time.

'The principle reason, as always, was the script,' said John, 'and Russell's first script was terrific. The phrase "a page-turner" comes immediately to mind. Once I started reading, I had to go right through to the end.

'The tenor of the piece is about Renard's moral dilemma: how can a priest get involved with one side or the other? You've got honourable men having to fight for their life, for their whole culture – in this case in France. For priests at that time, there were moral dilemmas, like hearing a confession when someone says: "I've just shot a German"; or someone who is pro-German, admitting: "I slept with a German last night." How does your conscience cope with that?'

Though John's most famous character, Morse, was at that time going about his sleuthing on French television, John was still able to enjoy a certain anonymity while on location in the picturesque fishing resort of St Valery-sur-Somme, in northern France. 'Years ago, *Morse* was shown on one of the major French channels,' John remembered, 'but now it was going out at lunchtime on a Sunday, which is exactly when no one in France is watching television! They're far too fond of their food for that.'

But he could not entirely escape the attention of unsuspecting visitors while filming. 'The town attracts a lot of French tourists, and, when I was making my way in costume through the streets from my caravan to the location, there would be a little nod of respect or acknowledgement to me as I walked past,' he noted. 'They didn't know I was simply an actor in a priest's robes.

'It was interesting that, when I put the vestments on, it did affect my demeanour. You have the history that goes with the part: you're aware of the people in the past who have worn this "uniform". And it also made me stand and walk in a certain way.'

The clothes John wore for Augustin Renard's church services actually belonged to the church of St Martin, which dominates the main square in the old part of town. 'They were very old and had been worn by many different priests,' John explained. 'I was aware as I stood in the pulpit, talking to the congregation, that the vestments could well have been worn in 1940 in that very pulpit.'

But it was not just the church vestments that brought back the reality of the past to John. 'Often, in the square outside the church, I would remember that here I was in the exact spot which had seen for real all the stuff we were doing fictionally. All I could do was stand there and wonder. Some of the older people watching us or living in the town had been through it all.'

According to John, some of the older residents of St Valery felt uneasy at the sight of German soldiers back on their streets and swastikas draped from public buildings. 'As you watched them walking to the shops, you felt they were rewinding to 1940,' John observed. 'You could almost read their minds. But they were so grateful for Britain's help during the war, they made a point of shaking your hand.

'Inevitably, though, old wounds were opened. I admit I felt humbled. One day an old lady shouted out at us and I was upset that she was upset. After all, when they were being occupied by the Germans, I was just a baby in Manchester.'

The reality of war in that part of France was brought home to John, not only by the fact that St Valery's square overlooks the Somme estuary, but that one side of the square had to have a specially built fourth wall of shops for the filming. Once there had been houses, but they were bombed accidentally by the British.

By coincidence, John knew that the production-design team of *Monsignor Renard* had the look of wartime St Josse

234

exactly right when he first returned to the set after a week-end spent narrating a Carlton TV documentary. John had been asked to voice the commentary for *The Second World War In Colour*, a task he began while still working on the French wartime drama. While working on the first episode of the documentary, he was fascinated to see the actual newsreel and then go back to the Renard set.

'It was so satisfying to see that we had got it right,' he said. 'I saw some of the shots of German-occupied France in the documentary and knew that, if you put them into *Monsignor Renard*, you wouldn't see any difference.'

John was typically dedicated in his preparation for his new role, voraciously reading books on the Occupation of France and immersing himself in videos of French films about that period.

And, before travelling to France to start filming, he met Father Kit Cunningham at St Ethelreda's in Holborn to learn precisely how a priest of that time would celebrate Mass. 'We videoed him, so that I could copy his actions exactly,' John said. 'And he even came out to France to check that I was getting it right! I'm not Catholic, so I had to learn how to be in the regalia and conduct the Latin mass.'

When the £6 million *Monsignor Renard* series reached TV screens in the spring of 2000, its launch was soured by the revelation that the series was to be axed after just four episodes on the grounds of cost. 'I'm very disappointed,' John admitted. 'The plan was to take the series from 1940 to the end of the war. But I'm a big boy and I can cope. That's the way this business goes sometimes. It's quality drama and I'm very pleased with what we have done.'

The producer, Chris Kelly, echoed John's feelings of discontent that the series was to end prematurely after Carlton TV deemed it too expensive to continue making it.

'It's the greatest part John has ever played in his TV career,' said Kelly, which was some accolade since he had collaborated with John on *Kavanagh QC*. 'It's compelling, entertaining and gripping, but apparently that's not enough. Where it ended – in 1940 – there were lots of loose ends. The Resistance hadn't even started by then. The idea was to make a series for each year of the war. John, as Renard, would go off to a concentration camp, which is where a lot of Catholic priests who resisted ended up. We were going to end with the liberation.'

Once again, as with *A Year in Provence*, crossing the channel for a series set in France had proved unlucky for John Thaw.

Nevertheless, he was determined to keep busy and followed up with *Buried Treasure*, a drama in which he played a hard-nosed businessman and golf-club captain who lives an extremely ordered life while rattling around alone in his huge detached house. Then the news that his estranged daughter has been killed in a road accident turns his life upside down: he discovers he has a granddaughter, Saffron, a strong-willed girl who needs him to look after her. He also played a former army intelligence officer in a two-part thriller, *The Waiting Time*.

The end of May 2001 saw John in his last major television project: *The Glass*, a six-part drama series about the world of selling, billed as 'a story of life, lust and betrayal'. It starred John as Jim Proctor, a self-made millionaire feared and respected by the employees of his window company, Albery Glass. In his fifties, Jim has a much younger girl-friend, the slim and beautiful Carol, played by Sarah Lancashire, and his decision to change his way of life undermines their relationship.

'He's concentrated on business and success for so long

he's forgotten how to interrelate with other people, not least Carol,' John explained. 'So he finds it very difficult to talk about his emotions and how he feels. He attempts to change no matter how clumsily and badly he might be going about it. But the good thing is he's conscious of his own defects as a human being, and is trying to do something about that.'

Sarah Lancashire, best known as the dizzy Weatherfield barmaid Raquel in Britain's premier soap *Coronation Street*, found herself falling under John's spell like so many of his female co-stars before her. 'I told John several times during filming how much I loved him and he just laughed it off,' she said. 'I can see why so many female viewers think he has such enormous sex appeal. He's charming, and sexy with it. The fact that he's of the same vintage as his character, and is therefore more than twenty years older than me is totally irrelevant. John, and at least some other men of that generation, have got to points in their lives where they don't have to prove themselves any more. They are happy within their skins and that's actually quite sexy. There's a confidence, ease and assurance about them which is enormously appealing.'

13

DEATH OF A MUCH-LOVED ACTOR

The terrible news broke in June 2001 that John Thaw had cancer of the oesophagus. His wife Sheila had known for some time that John was himself bravely fighting the deadly condition that had already ravaged his family. But a short statement was released to convey the dreadful news to the rest of the world:

> I am receiving treatment for cancer of the oesophagus. Sheila and I appreciate everyone's support and understanding but would now be very grateful if our privacy could be respected, particularly during the period of my treatment and recovery.

Typically, John said that, as soon as his medical treatment had been completed, he intended to return to work.

But cancer of the oesophagus, or gullet, affects about seven thousand people a year in Britain, and, while some are cured, usually with surgery, it is very hard to treat. John refused to bow down to the illness that had struck down his mother and his father. He resolved that he would undergo the treatment and he would return to work. At this time John drew enormous strength from his family and they were all greatly heartened by the deluge of messages of support from his faithful fans from all over the world.

John Thaw was always deeply moved by the impact of his work. He said that he was just doing a job and once it was over he liked to go home and forget about it, like anyone else. But he played roles with such searing compassion that they became part of people's lives. Many of those viewers who had enjoyed and been moved by his work took the time to send a letter of good wishes at this time and John and Sheila were greatly helped.

Tragically, eight months later, on 21 February 2002, John Thaw died at the family home at Luckington in Wiltshire. He was just sixty years old. And, even after the headline news that he was fighting cancer, it was still a massive shock. His close friend, the television executive Ted Childs, had been discussing John's return to work on a new adventure for Kavanagh QC only the week before. Ted, who worked with John as producer of *The Sweeney* and remained a trusted colleague and friend for more than thirty years, had had tea with John and Sheila and said sadly: 'John was just as he has been throughout his illness, positive, funny and self-effacing. Even in recent weeks when he clearly was not very well he was anxious to get back to work.'

On her 69th birthday Sheila released a sad statement:

> We have all been so grateful for the thousands of letters and messages wishing him well. Everyone has been wonderful during this difficult period and I would like them all to know how much their support and understanding meant to him and to all of us.

The tributes came thick and fast and with heartfelt sincerity. David Jason, that other great popular British television actor was clearly distressed by John's death. 'The man had a natural way with his ability as an actor,' said David. 'He found his way through to the centre of each character he played and he played them with tremendous sincerity. Everybody's going to remember him for Inspector Morse and I suppose I do, as well. But he did a wonderful piece recently called *Goodbye Mr Tom*. He was a real old rascal. And I thought that showed John Thaw probably in a much truer light because he reached inside himself.'

Lord (Richard) Attenborough recalled: 'I had the joy of getting to know John Thaw when I directed *Cry Freedom*. John won the Best Supporting Actor award at the BAFTAs and it can't have been more than three or four minutes. It was an exquisite piece of acting.'

Dennis Waterman remained a very close friend ever since their time together as Regan and Carter in *The Sweeney*. Dennis provided a real insight into the humanity of John Thaw when he said: 'I think the sex-symbol thing made him laugh a lot. It made me laugh a lot. For our four years on *The Sweeney* it was laughter all the time. We kept getting told off by the producer, who kept saying: "Will you stop laughing." We said: "Why? This is how we work." If you haven't heard John Thaw singing "The Sun Has Got His Hat On" while dancing on one of the squad office desks, you ain't heard nothing. The whole crew would be gone. He had a lovely sense of humour. I was not aware of the perfectionist side of him. We wanted to do well and we knew we were making a good programme. We just did the best we could and we just had the happiest time.'

Dennis will always be grateful for John's part in developing his share of *The Sweeney*: 'The absolute proof of John's generosity was that we became a double act. It was written for John. He *was* Regan. Then there is the sidekick. In the early episodes John was up there questioning people and I was standing there way behind and I might throw in a line here or there.

'After a while John said: "Hold on. You've got a really good actor here and all he's doing is standing behind me." He said: "Give him some of my lines." And he made us become a double act. And that is rare generosity in an actor. I always got children coming up and saying: "You're my mum's favourite. Will you sign this?" John got adults coming up and saying: "You're my favourite. Will you sign this?" And actresses would always be going on about those wonderful long eyelashes and those beautiful blue eyes. John found it hugely embarrassing. He didn't like all that stuff.'

Andy Allan was the programme boss at Central TV and Carlton TV who benefited most from John's remarkable ability to attract huge audiences for top-quality drama. Andy said: 'John will always be most strongly identified with *The Sweeney* and Morse, and yet, when you think about it, could you imagine two more different coppers?'

He continued: 'Because he was a deeply politically committed man he did have very strong egalitarian views about life. John insisted that he use his natural Manchester accent when he played Kavanagh QC. I think he wanted to put on telly the fact that a kid from Manchester could become a QC. I think that was important to him. Just by bringing that to the role he changed it from being a run-of-the-mill courtroom drama into a man involved in some sort of class-system fight against the establishment, and that's why a lot of people got on his side. And he instinctively knew that.

'It was terribly important to John that, whatever he was doing, when he was acting, there was an integrity there. He had to believe in the role. He was never one of those actors to whom you could just throw a part and he would act it. There had to be a lot of John in it. He was a great television actor. In those close-ups you could see behind the eyes into a man who could understand loneliness, but possibly more than loneliness: solitude – and be at ease with solitude.

'In the character I knew best, Inspector Morse, there was a lot of John, but that has often been described as a slightly ill-tempered curmudgeon. John was not that. John valued his privacy. What he brought to Morse was his intensity.'

The writer of the Inspector Morse novels, Colin Dexter, became a good friend of John's. Colin said: 'I think, to be truthful, that an awful lot of the ladies in the audience used to fall in love just slightly with John. They thought they would like to go out with him because he was a very inter-esting person, a striking individual as a man. I think perhaps the men thought more of him as a professional actor but I have met an awful lot of ladies who said he was their real pin-up boy.

'He was quite a shy person and a very private individ-ual,' Colin continued. 'He didn't long for all the publicity and queues of people waiting to see him. John Thaw told me on more than one occasion that he enjoyed playing Morse more than any other television role. He was a wonderfully gifted man with his patience and his profes-sionalism as a telly actor.'

Before John's death, the leading director Jack Gold, who made such a wonderful job of handling Morse's sad finale, said that he believed the extraordinary appeal of John Thaw lay in 'a combination of the smile, the opportunities for humour, the extraordinary blue eyes, I suppose, that make it all work. The attractiveness of John as Kavanagh comes from a combination of things. His own persona has a sort of gravitas about it. As a man he has lived in the world; he has family, he has children; he has cares and emotions; he has strong feelings about life and his attitudes to it. I think all those things bear on Kavanagh, who is a man, we believe, of integrity and humanity, and John has those so the man and the character are identified.'

Many of John Thaw's acting friends were devastated by his early death. And none more than Sir Tom Courtenay, who said: 'John and I met in 1960 when we were both students at the Royal Academy of Dramatic Art. I was twenty-one and he was only sixteen. He was very shy. And he looked frightening. Nobody dare talk to him. But being from a similar background I *did* dare talk to him. I didn't get a reply at first. There was something about him and we pretty soon became best pals.'

There was royal sympathy for the death of John Thaw. The Queen has long been an devotee of *Inspector Morse* since the programme's very early days. The American co-producer Rebecca Eaton, from WGBH in Boston, noted: 'Several years ago the Queen came to Washington, DC, for some reception for British TV in America. There was a giant party at the Library of Congress, and there was a long receiving line and several of us were being introduced. I was introduced as the American executive producer of the *Morse* series and her demeanour completely changed. She lit up like a Christmas tree and said: "*Morse*? Is he here?" '

Sarah Lancashire, who starred with John Thaw in the ITV serial *The Glass*, said he was a 'national treasure' and would be greatly missed. 'It was a privilege to have worked with John but an even greater one to have known him, albeit briefly, as a friend,' she said.

Kevin Whately played Morse's faithful sidekick Sergeant Lewis in 32 of the 33 films and the two men forged a strong friendship. Kevin recalled his very first meeting with John

Thaw: 'I'd been asked to read for this new series of three films called *Inspector Morse*. I was working in rep and barely knew John's work. I'd never even seen *The Sweeney*.

'John came into this tiny room and we read together. I remember these steely blue eyes, looking up over his script all the time and weighing me up. I knew straightaway that he was very quiet; he was always very friendly, but it took a long time to get to know John.

'We shared a caravan on *Morse*, as he had done with Dennis in *The Sweeney*. On the first ever day's filming, we were at Bray Studios. I remember his incredibly fierce concentration. It could be quite scary. I remember seeing other young actors coming in later on and being affected by this. But John loved doing the work and that concentration came out of that; it was all important to get it right. You quickly fell in with it. We used to sit in the caravan and talk about the scenes before we did them so I knew where I was coming from; but, if somebody was coming in new, you could be quite taken aback by it.

'After a couple of months I got to know John and could relax, and he was the best company you could have. He was great fun. He loved it when we found a new writing talent. He was a great defender of writers as well. Most actors will look at a difficult sentence and think, That's hard for me to say, and ask the director if they can change it into their own words. John would never do that. He would always imagine the writer sitting at home all night typing away. He would say the writer knows exactly what he meant there and it's our job as actors to work it out.

'He was full of funny stories and a very affectionate friend. He was a very loyal person. We felt very close when we were working. My fondest memories are of sitting in the caravan at the end of a long day. If we had had a real "beast" of a scene, when we were very aware of how each other was "suffering" at different times in those scenes, I loved sitting with John and talking to him. Without exactly saying "Congratulations, we did that", that was the atmosphere in the caravan.

'He was a huge acting talent. He was a very hard worker, and he was very self-deprecating. When he got his CBE, for weeks after that he would make jokes. Whenever he found himself in a slightly undignified position on the set or he had to say something awkward in the script he would say: "I can't say this – I'm a Commander of the British Empire!"

'John had a wonderful sense of humour, which is belied sometimes by journalists' impression of him as irascible. He loathed the whole celebrity circuit. In between takes he was like an Irish storyteller in a bar: he wouldn't tell jokes, just stories, and you would find yourself rolling around and crying with laughter. He was a wonderful mimic, particularly of people on the set rather than famous people. He would pick up a director's little tics very fast.'

Kevin cannot recall that the two ever had a bad word in fifteen years of working very closely together. 'We did have a lot in common in that we are similarly shy and not showbizzy types. But I wish I had half his acting talent. I'm a workaday working actor, but John had an extra dimension to his work which very few actors in Britain have.'

John Thaw's funeral was a private family affair. No stars attended the rain-swept Westerleigh crematorium outside Bristol on 25 February. Sheila and their daughters Melanie, Abigail and Joanna led a dozen mourners at the quiet service. John's son-in-law, Matthew Byam, said the family had been overwhelmed by letters and messages of sympathy, and explained: 'Sheila is exhausted after caring for John and devastated by his death, so the service was very private. When the family has gathered its strength again a celebration of John will be arranged.'

EPILOGUE

John Thaw was much more emotional than fans of *The Sweeney* or *Inspector Morse* would believe. He was very sentimental, very sensitive. All sorts of things made him sad: films of horrific famines in Africa reduced him to tears; he cried when he heard John Lennon had died.

John knew that having a motherless childhood had made a subconscious difference to the caring yet easygoing way he has brought up his children. But the scars of his mother's agonizing exit from his life and the memories of his painful time at RADA faded with the years. Since his reconciliation with Sheila, after their brief split, the couple enjoyed a very happy relationship.

Yet he still found it hard to handle the endless attention that came with television success. His brother Ray, who regularly kept in touch in spite of their vastly different lifestyles, certainly did not envy John's stardom. Ray knows John as a very quiet person who didn't like socializing.

When John visited him in Australia Ray invited his brother down to his local pub for a drink. John didn't want to go for fear of being recognized, but his brother assured him no one would bother him, so off they went. They had hardly walked into the bar before someone said, 'You're that bloke from *The Sweeney*,' and that was the end of that. John's shyness and desire for privacy is one thing his brother had a go at him about. 'I once said to him, "You're in show business, you should face up to it." But he replied he just wanted to do his job and be left alone. There's nothing he likes more than to grab a book, listen to classical music and basically lounge around. He is not like the sort of actor who wants star treatment as soon as they get a name. He's not into that.'

John's shyness was the reason why he hated to appear on TV talk shows. On one of the few occasions he agreed to be interviewed it was only after Sir Richard Attenborough begged him to accompany him. John admitted to Ray: 'I was very nervous because I don't like to talk about Mum and stuff like that.'

While John Thaw was remarkably quiet and reserved, he was anything but mean. Ray said: 'He is very generous and always says to me, "If you're in strife or you need something you've only got to phone me," but obviously we try not to do that.' When their father was alive John would have done anything to make his life easier. 'I've seen him offer dad cars, but he always said "No," ' said Ray.

His brother's verdict on John is: 'Obviously John enjoys the rewards but from what I've seen you can keep his lifestyle. Once John told me, "Ray, you go to work and you go home at the end of the day and there is no hassle. That is what I want with my job." '

The constant recognition was something even the new, more mellow John Thaw found hard to live with: 'I do try hard to make having a famous face and getting recognized all over the place feel part of the job. But I'm afraid I'm a slave to my moods. So if I'm not feeling particularly happy and joyful I don't like being greeted by people saying,

"Cheer up, John. It may never happen!" I just want to be totally free like they are to walk around unrecognized. If they want to look lost, or happy, or sad, or whatever nobody gives a damn. That's their business. But because I am seen on telly I've got to suffer all the crap, so that irritates me.

'I never wanted to be recognized, that was not why I went off to RADA to try to become an actor. I have always thought of acting as another job. I don't believe it's anything special but the fame makes it different. And I have always had problems coping with the recognition that success brings, with being John Thaw the actor as opposed to John Thaw the person. They seem to me two totally different people and two different things. One is a job I can do and the other is me the human being like you, or the bus driver or the guy that reads the gas meter. I can't put John Thaw the actor and John Thaw the person together. That's why I can come off the set after a highly charged scene and make a joke because what I've just done is my job, and afterwards I'm the real me. A lot of people have married the two together but I struggle to do it. I'm better than I was, a lot better. But I'm still trying.'

When the family home was near the River Thames in Chiswick the neighbours learned not to bother the shy Mr Thaw. 'They all knew me and they didn't bother me. They'd just say "Hello John" and if they can see I don't want to stop and hear how their holidays were then they'd leave me alone. In other places they sometimes come up and ask if I'm John Thorp, or as one Irishman put it "John Throw-up". Perhaps he was just making a comment on my last performance.

'I know people are mostly very nice and they generally just want to say they enjoy *Morse* or whatever, but when a crowd of strangers stares at me I always feel as though I've got three heads. Sometimes they pretend they haven't seen you but another thing that irritates me all the time is the way some people in shops or department stores behave. They clock you and then tip the wink to whoever they're with and then they follow you round, trying to pretend they're looking for something in the shop. I'll be in Marks and Spencer and they're at the end of the aisle giving me sidelong glances and I can see they're wondering why I've got baggy trousers on or whatever.

'Sheila feels the same way about attention as I do but being basically a much wiser person than me she accepts it is part of the job. She says to me it is much better to appear as if you don't mind rather than behave as I sometimes do and snap and snarl.

'If Sheila is swamped by a hundred people wanting autographs and they ignore me that's fine. I'm delighted, thank you very much. My usual trick is to walk away and to pretend I'm not with her. When we go to dos together and come out and find fans wanting autographs or to take our picture, a lot of them rush to Sheila and a lot rush to me, and I hurriedly do mine and then walk off smartly. Sometimes she looks up and finds I'm a hundred yards up the road. And that can annoy her. But I just think it's great if they surround Sheila, I'll leg it now.

'Being recognized all the time does get on my nerves. When we lived in Chiswick we used to go for a walk on the towpath and if it was a sunny day with loads of people about I would get to the point where I was being stared at so much and subjected to so much nudge-nudge, wink-wink attention that I would think, "To hell with it, I'd much sooner go and walk round the bloody garden. It's just not worth the aggravation." '

But John insisted he had come to terms with the penalties of the level of popularity that most actors would sell a close relative for. 'I don't wake up in the morning and think, "Oh God. People are going to stare at me today."' He laughed. 'It really is just occasionally that it gets to me. But that is why it is so wonderful going abroad to France or Italy where I can wander around unrecognized. It's a fantastic feeling of freedom that I love. As long as it's off the beaten track of British tourists I can walk down the street without anyone giving me a second glance.'

The biggest recent tragedy in John Thaw's life was the death from cancer of his father in 1997. John was very close to him all his life. Of course they were pushed together with brother Raymond when his mother left home, but John remained devoted to the end. He knew how faithfully his father supported him through his life, how he fought for him to go to the right school, how he helped him get to RADA. And how he put his own life on hold until John and Raymond were settled.

To the end John and Sheila made many trips north to try to help care for John senior. He loved being taken out for a meal by his famous son and daughter-in-law. And when John's busy work schedule meant he could not see his father in person he telephoned every day.

In spite of his three lovely homes and his gleaming Jaguar, John lived an essentially simple life. He preferred plain English food and loved to spend his free time out of the public gaze, either pottering in his beautiful Wiltshire garden or indoors listening to his beloved classical music.

His taste in women had not changed. John said: 'I like intelligent women. I put intelligence before anything. I've worked with some very attractive ladies but I don't see that beauty unless they are bright. Oh yes, they've got to have a sense of humour, too.' Fortunately for him, Sheila Hancock and his daughters qualify on all counts.

Most of all he would have loved to do his job and somehow remain anonymous. And he has very definite views on publicity. During one *Morse* interview he said: 'I don't have to do this. I think you're quite a pleasant chap to spend an evening with, but I know that when I stopped doing interviews for a whole series the figures went up and I won an award. I thought, "There's a moral in there somewhere." I have realized that publicity and giving interviews are not actually very important. Earlier in my career I thought, "God, I ought to do this." Now I think, "No, I don't want to talk about myself because I know it doesn't matter one jot. It doesn't matter to the programme, to my life or my career if I was not here now."

'Sheila says that in America publicity is still thought of as part of the job for an actor and they do anything to get it. If you get the chance to talk to the *Arkansas Gazette* then you do it. With the British, I think that is less and less necessary.

'And some shows get so much publicity that when they come on the programme is a bit of an anti-climax. When I played Francis Drake for Westward Television it was the biggest thing they had ever done, but it was also the last thing they ever did. It broke the bank. It was well directed and well acted and it won a couple of prizes but there had been so much advance publicity – me on boats and me playing bowls – that when it came out you wouldn't have known it was on. The journalists didn't mind. They'd had great trips down on location to Plymouth and got themselves rat-arsed in the Holiday Inn. We all had a good laugh but it didn't do the programme any good.

'Look at this nonsense when I was supposed to be the

man most women would like to have a dirty weekend with! I didn't know anything about that and yet it was splashed all over the tabloids. Then Radio 1 got in on the act and my name was all over that. Of all places! It's just silly crap. The research for the weekend was sponsored by a travel company who specialized in weekends, would you believe. My missus laughed and said a dirty weekday would suit me!'

Despite his promises to take life easy John Thaw remained a driven man, who loved to throw himself into his work. John always tried to give 100 per cent to any job he did. Partly it was his working-class upbringing coming out. An honest day's work for an honest day's pay. Partly it was the inbuilt insecurity of an actor that evidently never leaves you, always concerned about where the next job is coming from no matter how many millions you have in the bank. But John listened and learned as his career went on. He always remembered appearing in a play directed by Lindsay Anderson in which he was off-stage for an extended period. The play involved a chorus of about half a dozen firemen and Anderson asked him to come on with the chorus, apparently because he didn't like the idea of his staying in his dressing room doing nothing. Thaw was reluctant, but the acclaimed director explained that if he had asked Peter O'Toole to do it, *he* would have agreed and then made absolutely sure he was the very best fireman on stage. Thaw got the message and says that since then he has put maximum effort into everything he has done.

John always tried to have the same team of people around him. His driver, his make-up man and his wardrobe man all worked with him for years. Loyalty was very important and John trusted his little group implicitly.

He preferred to mix with familiar faces. With them, there was no competition, they were on his side. He could go back to his caravan and talk about his kids, their kids, Manchester United and make jokes. But he liked nothing to get in the way of the work.

Sheila understood the compulsion. After all, it was work which brought them together in the first place. But the couple were anything but typical luvvies who spent hours moaning about the size of their billing. John said: 'We only discuss work to moan, not how to play a scene or a character. Like any couple, we just grumble about what a hard day it's been or gossip about what so and so said.'

With their children off their hands and busy raising their own families, John and Sheila seem happier than ever. John said: 'We have similar tastes in music. I think about ninety per cent of what I like, she likes. I have introduced Sheila to a lot of music that she didn't know but now loves more passionately than me. When we first got together she was more famous than me but now I think she's grateful that sometimes she is not recognized in some places. There has never been any rivalry between us, it has never entered my mind and I'm pretty sure it has never entered Sheila's either.'

John Thaw and Sheila Hancock had over a quarter of a century of marriage behind them, and their relationship was rock solid. John said: 'Sheila is working on a novel. I don't know where she gets the energy or the time, but she has always been an early riser. She finds she can really concentrate while I'm still asleep. Somehow she finds time to do it before eight o'clock in the morning.

'Her health seems OK, thank goodness. The cancer is in remission. But we just try to take each day as it comes. She is a remarkable woman and I know I am very, very lucky to have her.'

John Thaw had the kind of irresistible audience appeal that could earn him more than £1 million a year and a luxury lifestyle with beautiful homes in both England and France. But he began life in circumstances that were anything but glamorous. 'I have come a long way from my roots,' he said simply. 'I had a lot of luck and a gift I was given at birth. Acting was the only thing I could do.'